MW00976828

Dear
Mr. Johnson,

Thank you for all
the wonderful moments
I have had the pleas...
to spend with you.

All my best,

Jose
Salinas.

HOMER'S BLIND AUDIENCE

An essay on the Iliad's *geographical prerequisites for the site of Ilios.*

HOMER'S BLIND AUDIENCE

An essay on the Iliad's *geographical prerequisites for the site of Ilios.*

by

ROBERTO SALINAS PRICE

SCYLAX PRESS, INC.

Copyright © 1983 by
Scylax Press, Inc.
P. O. Drawer 1340
San Antonio, Texas 78295

All rights reserved.
No part of this book may be reproduced or transmitted in any form or by
any means, electronic or mechanical, including photocopying, recording or
by any information storage and retrieval system, without permission in
writing from the Publisher.

Library of Congress Cataloging in Publication Data

Salinas-Price, Roberto,   1936-
  Homer's blind audience.
  Includes index.
  1. Homer. Iliad.   2. Troy (Ancient city)   3. Dalmatia (Croatia) in literature.   4. Dalmatia (Croatia)—Antiquities.   I. Title.
        PA4037.S24   1984   883'.01   83–20342

ISBN 0-910865-10-8

Scylax means 'a young dog, a whelp, puppy.' It is derived from the Greek
verb *scyllo*, 'to flay: to rend, mangle, tear' (and metaphorically, 'to trouble,
annoy'), as young pups are wont to do with whatever they put their paws
on.

Scylax is also the name of an ancient geographer from Caryanda, mentioned by Herodotus as an explorer for Darius I (521–486 B.C.), and quoted
centuries later by Strabo in his geography of the Troad. Nothing certain
remains of his work, but a fourth century *Periplus* is a compilation in
his name.

Therefore, it has seemed apt to use the picture of the Pompeian mosaic
depicting a chained dog with the inscription CAVE CANEM, 'beware of the
dog,' as a trademark for Scylax Press.

The symbolism is in the literary guardianship, and defense of, the validity
of geographical information in the Homeric Writings, as if to warn explor-
ing ships on the sea of classics of perilous straits before safe entry into port.

TABLE OF CONTENTS:

PART V

Preface

The sole purpose of this book is to focus on a novel approach to the age-old Homeric Question. It would seem that if the enormous talent of modern classical scholarship has come to an insuperable impass regarding this issue, then something is seriously out of kilter. But perhaps the specialist in Homeric scholarship will not admit there is any such thing as an impass regarding the Homeric Question, and dismiss the matter altogether. Yet the fact is—as the reader will learn—scholarship pertinent to the Homeric Question is yielding nothing of substance.

The statement I have made is simple: Troy was not in Asia Minor; Troy was in Yugoslavia. Consequently, many serious questions, and twice as many conclusions derived from such a premise (which I call the Homeric Position), have arisen. But I must necessarily leave these unanswered, else the scope of the book be altered. Nevertheless, I like to think that, at least, I have raised an important issue and suggested a chronological model—a paradigm—on which other investigators may follow-up, and build on their own, an historical picture of the proto-historic times of our Western Civilization.

I also like to think this book is entirely, like the White Night said, ". . . my own invention," from conception, research, writing, proofing, editing, and finally, publishing. But alas! it was not to be so. Such accomplishments are rare, and along the way many dear friends have willy-nilly intruded upon my efforts with their valuable contributions towards a final product. So to all, many, many thanks are due for their enthusiasm—and more, for their love and their loyalty. Paramount

among them, are my wife Marie Linda and my children Robby and
Marilí, who have taxed me so heavily with my commitment that they
may, at last, be very proud of a book such as I wrote.

Now, the issue of a bibliography has come up: Dr. William Samelson
and his lovely wife Rosa Salinas Samelson (not a relative), whose opin-
ions I respect, have finally given their approval of this book. But, they
have insisted that a bibliography (which I was loath to include) be
listed. My argument to them was that since the premise of my thesis
breaks radically from the current trends of Homeric scholarship, bibli-
ographicl references could only serve the purpose of embarrassing the
professionalism of other Homeric scholars, a thing which is not in my
nature to do, and was unwilling to undertake. But Billy and Rosita
were very clever in their counter-argument that I could not, in all good
faith, write about the futility of current Homeric scholarship without
at least giving the reader the benefit of some idea of *where* it has erred.
So, I have compromised, and rather than listing a bibliography in the
accustomed manner of citing sources for my statements, I have given
a list of those authoritative books which more or less represent the
general consensus of current Homeric scholarship.

Lastly, the reader should be told that the companion volume (or se-
quel) to this book is *The Odysseus Manuscript*, which is about Aristid
S. Vucetic's discovery in 1935 that the Wanderings of Odysseus occurred in the Adriatic Archipelago, off the Trojan coast. The argument
and substance of Vucetic's work came to me too late (though I had been
superficially acquainted with it since 1967) to modify the original plan
of this publication and incorporate here.

Since the *Odyssey*, it could be said, is the other half of the *Iliad* (for
in geographical terms, the *Iliad* treats largely with information about
peoples and places abroad, whereas the *Odyssey* is confined to giving a
considerable amount of information about the Trojan seaboard), *The
Odysseus Manuscript* is relevant to what is here mentioned about
Troy's geography. And conversely, what is mentioned here about Troy's
geography is relevant to a better understanding of the *Odyssey's* true
scenario along the Trojan seaboard.

San Antonio, Texas.   Roberto Salinas Price
Autumn, 1984.

PART I

CHAPTER 1

THE *ILIAD*

The study of the *Iliad* is not for the impatiently prose-minded, for it is
fraught with such enormous difficulties that one may only conjure
truths from it (for the satisfaction of giving the Muse a wink) with the
greatest of diligence.

Principal among these difficulties, is the task of reconciling the text's
various geographical and topological references to the environs of Ilios,
with the incongruity of the existing features in the landscape surrounding the Trojan countryside. The reader of the *Iliad* perceives the
narration is set within a geography of its own peculiar making, but
attempts to understand it as a whole, or clarify doubts about the location of certain sites, show a geography which rarely comes into contact
with the reality of the world. In fact, the difficulty is so great, that one
must eventually arrive at some sort of compromise, for what the *Iliad*
says, and what one finds, are two different things.

For instance, it is not clear whether the narration opens on one of the
islands near the mainland (most likely Tenedos) and then moves onto
the mainland for the continuation of the account, thus leaving one at
odds as to how Achilles, who at the beginning had withdrawn from the
entire enterprise, is later found to be visited by king Priam himself. Or,
whether the account of the siege on Ilios opens already on the mainland thus accounting for Achilles' visit by king Priam, but putting the
Danaans' assault on Trojan soil via a naval approach out of kilter with
a fluent sequence of events.

The problem of relating the story of the *Iliad* with the terrain of Troy
is compounded further by the very disquieting fact that none of the

descriptions of Ilios given in the text—and the details that might be inferred from them—can be seen in the archaeological stratum of Hissarlik labeled TROY VIIb2. Furthermore, not only is an anachronism worked into the estimated date for this stratum and that of the Trojan War, but also a gross discrepancy between its destruction by earthquake and the traditional accounts of its destruction by looting and fire.

Witness the following ambiguity—or the difficulty with precision—in a description of the Trojan plain in J. V. Luce's *Homer and the Heroic Age* (Thames and Hudson, 1975, Chap. 6, p. 124):

> . . . the Dumbrek is to be identified with the Simoeis. It has its own small alluvial plain running back along the northern flank of the ridge that ends at Hisarlik [*sic*], and it finds its way to the sea at the eastern edge of the beach that lies between the ridges of Sigeum and Rhoeteum.[4] This beach was an obvious landing-point for a seaborne expedition coming to attack Troy, and is the generally accepted location for the Greek camp.[5]

The footnotes at the end of the chapter read:

> 4. The Sigeum ridge was probably the site of the earthworks of Herakles from which the gods on the Achaean side watched the battle. South and east of Rhoeteum stands the prominent hill Kara Tepe, probably to be identified with Homer's Kallikolone which served as a grandstand for the gods favouring the Trojans (*Iliad* 20, 144–52). For the most recent discussion of the topography and identifications see J. M. Cook, *The Troad: an archaeological and topographical study* (Oxford 1973), 110–13, 165–9.
>
> 5. It is hard to see why Cook, *Troad*, 171 stigmatizes the beach at the north end of the Trojan plain as 'an impossible camping site'. The alternative which he appears to favour, without actually committing himself, is Besika Bay, but this hypothesis raises many more difficulties than it solves.

To my knowledge, the most authoritative and up-to-date work on the topography of Troy is J.M. Cook's *The Troad*. It would be difficult to supersede the author's first-hand knowledge of the environs of Hissarlik, yet one need only glance through this extensively documented work to see that it is a monumental testimony to the enormous difficulties encountered in identifying the *Iliad's* landscape with the existing terrain. To wit, he says the following (ch. 4, p. 91):

> The difficulty with Homer is that of knowing what truth there is in his facts, figures and topographical clues. And this difficulty is so serious that on a strict view of the matter it could be said that to the modern topographer of the ancient Trojan Plain he is not a primary source. His value is an indirect one. In general, the ancient scholars who concerned themselves with Trojan topography regarded Homer as historically accurate and believed that anything that conflicted with his account must be false; and consequently the text of Homer is an essential control for the understanding of their arguments. But we cannot do more than recognize what the ancient scholars pointed out as the Homeric topographical features.

Ever since the composition of the *Iliad* and the *Odyssey*, the slow —but inexorable—wheels of progress have brought them to us through generation upon generation of scholars who have shed some light, some perspective, some opinion on them. How they were not lost to us forever, and have survived the impious frays of our Western Civilization, is not a miracle. It is simply because, ever since their composition, scholars have treasured them far more than any other treasure.

So, one could say, that in a special way, there is really very little which is new in the study of the *Iliad* and the *Odyssey*. Ideas beget ideas, and so it is difficult to think of one generation of scholars as bearing no influence upon the next. The full blossom of one idea contains the seed of another that will flourish later, given the proper leisurely conditions. It is in this regard that a unique milestone in Homeric scholarship was Heinrich Schliemann's discovery in the 1880's of the numerous strata at Hissarlik.[1] Prior to this time, even from antiquity, there had been arguments for or against several proposed sites for the location of Homeric Ilios. Strabo himself, with whom it is generally agreed the study of Homeric geography begins, proposed an alternate location for the site of Homeric Ilios than the one then called Ilion (the uppermost stratum of Hissarlik, labeled TROY IX). But the transcendental significance of Schliemann's discovery is that

---

1. It is a shame Heinrich Schliemann's name is associated with ignominy, for as bungling an archaeologist as he was, and as dubious as the reports of his findings were, these still cannot diminish the underlying romance of his passions, nor the conquest of his goals.

the *Iliad* and the archaeological importance of the site of Hissarlik were to be inextricably bonded to each other. At last, it seemed as though the historical germ of the *Iliad* was attested to by the scientific evidence of these ruins. And the centuries-old tradition of Homeric scholarship became fused, or streamlined—as if finally corroborated by these ruins—for, indeed, Hissarlik has become the point of contact between the illusory world of the *Iliad* and the historical framework of reality.

It had already been reasoned before Schliemann's time that the story of a siege, and all its sundry details, had been woven out of the accounts of local folklore. These accounts were thought to have developed gradually and independently, over the centuries, through an oral transmission from one generation to the next, until somehow, in some mysterious way, they finally gelled in what became the singular literary accomplishment of all time.[2] But after Schliemann's discovery, Homeric scholarship (which in itself is quintessential to broader spectra of classical studies) was unable to think of the *Iliad* as anything other than the result of an evolutionary process, and this agravated all the conundrums enveloped withthin the *Iliad's* factual sense.

The assumed oral evolution of the *Iliad* into the final form which Monro *et* Allen have given in their Oxford Classical Text is thought to account for some of its internal inconsistencies. Factual mistakes and poetic licences are merely thought of as accommodating the fundamental needs of good narrative poetry, albeit not important to the overall picture of the narration's historical picture. Paradoxically, in as much as the *Iliad* is unequivocally regarded as the supreme authority on Troy,. only certain calculated and often intricate conclusions can be drawn from the study of its geographical information.

It is *precisely* because the *Iliad* became positively associated with the fortress of Hissarlik that Homeric scholarship has become sterile, yielding little towards a clearer or wider understanding of Homeric times or of pre-Homeric societies. Homeric scholarship—indeed, classical scholarship in general—has unwittingly fallen into an impass from which it has not recovered, for the only forward strides since Schliemann's discovery have been, on the one hand, the formation of a proto-historical picture of Hellas and, on the other, the development of methodological applications to the study of the Homeric Writings.

---

2. The thesis of the mechanics of an oral transmission was put forward as the only viable means of accounting for how such a composition could have come into existence, in the absence of evidence that could possibly substantiate a knowledge of writing at that time.

But returning to Strabo's preoccupation with the site of Homeric Ilios (the reader should be advised that he held Homer in great esteem), an idea which has not been adequately exploited is that, *if* the *Iliad* is a valid document whose information *is* reliable, then the archaeological evidence retrieved from Hissarlik must surely qualify as reasonable evidence that the site was simply not the Ilios described in the *Iliad*.

Where, then, is Ilios?

CHAPTER 2

THE HOMERIC SITE OF ILIOS

A basic assumption about the *Iliad* is that the story of the siege of Ilios is set in the environs of Hissarlik, in the northwestern corner of Asia Minor.

It is not.

The *Iliad* is set in Dalmatia, in the delta-valley of the Neretva river which debouches into the Adriatic, north of Dubrovnik and south of Split. The site of Ilios is to be identified with the small town of Gabela situated on a three-spurred, *trinacría*-shaped hillock (a three-legged, sun-faced device) located about twenty-two kilometers up-stream from the river's estuary.

The *Iliad's* narration cannot be assigned to another location (not successfully, at least) as it is otherwise wholly lost to the reader.[1] Simply, no other site can satisfy the intricacies of the geographical prerequisites for the site of Ilios, though in a general way, these prerequisites are, in Asia Minor, much the same as those to be found in Dalmatia: a sea in the west peppered with islands; a plain beside the sea; a mighty river; cloud-banked mountain peaks; and so on. But a diligent study of the *Iliad's* geography, on a comparative basis, will show these prerequisites are seriously wanting and utterly incompatible with Hissarlik and its environs.

Gabela has some 750 inhabitants; the town is spread mid-way along the southeastern length of its three spurs, and a road runs through it from the plain up to the western and northern spurs, and in the opposite direction, to a hill at the end of the southeastern spur.

The western spur is the highest of the three. The summit is topped by an oval stone platform of neolithic origins, and superimposed on it are the remains of a look-out post, perhaps of Roman or Turkish origins. In the center of the platform is the small church of Sveti Stephan, whose name appears to have been inspired by the platform's *crown*-like effect about the apex of the summit. Beside the platform, in the shade of a pine grove, is the local cemetery.

The northern spur, just below the height of the western, is topped by the remains of a massive, L-shaped construction in several terraced levels. A circular tower dating from the times of the Turkish domination is incorporated into the construction at one of the corners, and the stone lintel in the door-way is incised with a date that appears to read + 11 . 1.[2]

The southeastern spur slopes down to a few meters above the plain, and continues to the sudden rise of the third and lowest of the three heights. This height is surrounded by a fortress-like, almost rectangular, stone wall and tower, and within the more or less level enclosure are set the remains of ruined ivy-covered buildings. Here too, they are perhaps of Roman or Turkish origins. By contrast with the dry and arid northern and western spurs, the southeastern is humid, and hedged with trees and lush vegetation along the perimeter of the walls.

This is Ilios.

The ruins of its former existence are still preserved in the present lay-out of Gabela, and their descriptions were recorded by Homer (ostensibly, in the state he saw them some time after the Trojan War) with sufficient detail to identify them from the text (which cannot be said about TROY VIIb2).[3]

The name of Gabela is derived from the Italian *gabella* meaning 'a tax' or 'duty,' and comes from the times during the Dubrovnik Republic (1358–1809) when the town was the centre of a salt market, and went

1. An example of how the setting of the *Iliad* in its correct geographical context enhances the narration beyond its current appreciation can be seen in the following chapter, in the instance where Agamemnon offers Achilles 'seven well-peopled cities.'

2. There is difficulty in ascertaining whether the date is Christian or Muslim: 1,101 A.D. seems too early, and though 1,686 of the Hejira seems likelier, there is no satisfactory explanation to account for the Christian cross before a Muslim date. The tower may be ascribed to the Turkish builder Kodža Mustapaša Ušćuplija.

3. The innuendo is that Homer—or those responsible for the *Iliad's* authorship—were Trojan peoples who survived the ravages of the Trojan War and wrote about it at a later time. This is more in keeping with an ancient tradition about Homer himself having been present during the war, than with the current thesis of local folklore evolving into the formal rigors of a full-fledged epic through an oral transmission from generation to generation.

under the name of Drijeva; presumably, the prefix *dri-* echoes the hillock's *three* spurs.

The Neretva, formerly the Italian Narenta, derived its name from the Latin Naro. It was evidently so called because its headwaters in the hinterland mountains were thought to rise from *two* sources; or, because the Naro marshes flanking the river at its estuary (whence the name of the Roman town of Narona, today Vid, on a low hill on the west side of the marshes was also derived) were each drained by *two* small river systems. The Norino (a broken-down diminutive form) drains the marshes of the west, and the Krupa those of the east. The association of 'two' with the name Naro is through the Latin *nares*, 'nostrils' (like that of the Rhine with the Greek *rhis*, 'nose,' which also rises at *two* sources), and hence offers an apt connotation of the two unhealthy marshes with fetid nasal mucus. In the name of Naro then, is a vestige of the Trojan river Simoïs, meaning 'snub-nosed,' which

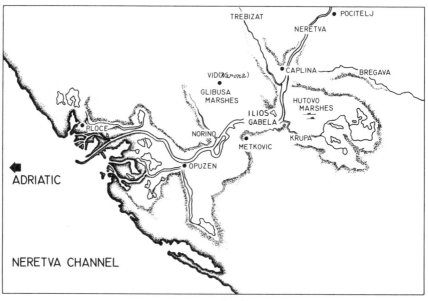

The site of Ilios, now Gabela, located where the Neretva turns in a generally western flow, is flanked by marshes which the geographer Scylax confused for a lake and the source of the Naro. In ancient times the river was navigable as far as Počiteli. Today, small cargo vessels go as far inland as Metković.

flowed into Scamander near Ilios from the east; it was so called because it drained two distinct lake areas separated by a spit.

Differences of opinion as to the exact location of the Homeric Ilios, and the intended location of various other places are well attested to, yet, while these per se are important allusions to the *Iliad's* true setting in Dalmatia, almost nothing is extant in classical literature to indicate an explicit reference to the Homeric antecedents of the area in question. Often, anything that sounds like an allusion on which to build a case is too tenuous and requires a prior working-knowledge of basic Homeric geography to be understood in that context.

If one turns to classical literature for ancient references to this area, in search of hints and to learn what was known about its history, one cannot be too certain that the entire canon of Greek classical literature unanimously endorsed the historicity of the popular Asia Minor Ilios. Nor, on the otherhand, that the historical importance of the *Iliad's* correct setting in a Dalmatian context escaped the attention of a discerning intellectual, and went unrecorded.

Consequently, whatever information may be sought in ancient sources is, in a sense, oblique at this time and yields nothing in the order of clarity; at most, its indirect nature constitutes an argument external to the *Iliad*, and can only suggest that it was once a well known fact to the intelligentsia of former times, that Ilios, as represented by the stratum of TROY VIII at Hissarlik,[4] was a bogus site—a boorish fabrications—that could not hold up adequately to the scrutiny of the text which celebrated it.

But the difficulty of interpreting Greek and Latin classical authors whose works are directly or indirectly relevant to the Troy theme, is that they are culturally pervaded by the popular tradition of an Asia Minor Ilios. This tradition became so ingrained in Troy's historical legacy, that it is difficult, and extremely tedious, to lend their works any sort of geographical harmony with a Dalmatian context. An example is to be seen in Strabo who describes the following about the Troad in his *Geography*, XII, 1, 34:

> . . . the two plains above mentioned are separated from each other by a great neck of land which runs in a straight line between the aforesaid spurs, starting from the present Ilium,

---

4. TROY VIII is the stratum representing the Greek colonization of the Hellespont, circa 720–700 B.C., some five hundred years *after* the estimated date for the events of the Trojan War.

with which it is connected, and stretches as far as Cebrenia and, along with the spurs on either side, forms a complete letter E [epsilon].

True, the marsh plains of the Neretva delta-valley seem as though they are contained by the hillside contours of a letter epsilon, but is Strabo not playing with his reader and intending instead "a complete letter Y [upsilon]," which is precisely the shape of Ilios?

Another case is Strabo's account of how the Neaethus river, now the Neto, north of Crotone, in Calabria, got its name (VI; 1, 12):

> Certain of the Achaeans who had strayed from the Trojan fleet put in there and disembarked for an inspection of the region, and when the Trojan women who were sailing with them learned that the boats were empty of men, they set fire to the boats, for they were weary of the voyage, so that the men remained there of necessity, although they at the same time noticed that the soil was very fertile. And immediately several other groups, on the strength of their racial kinship, came and imitated them, and thus arose many settlements, most of which took their names from the Trojans; and also a river, the Neaethus, took its apellation from the aforementioned occurrence.

Neas aethion means 'to burn ships,' and hence the name of the river; a look at a good road map of Calabria will show the tiny town of Gabella Grande between Crotone and the mouth of the Neto. A coincidence? Maybe.

However, there is one succinct statement—the only one that I know of—in a comment on Stephanos of Byzantium, a 10th century geographer, which clearly contests the popular tradition of an Asia Minor Ilios in favor of a location in Europe; it is to be found in Movses Dasxurançi's[5] *History of the Caucasian Albanians*, III, 18, (London: Oxford University Press, 1961, translated by C.J.F. Dowsett) and reads as follows:

> *In the books of Step'annos there is to be found an account of the destruction of Ilion and the building of Rome.*
>
> In the days of Abdan the Judge Ilion was taken as follows. This city was in the land of the Achaeans adjacent to the

---

5. Also called Kalankatuaçi.

Peloponnese west of Macedonia in the land of Europe . . . In
those days a certain young man from among the princes of the
city went to the town of Thessalonika, which is in the east of
Macedonia, in search of diversion, and was received by the
nobles of the town . . .

The account continues through the story of the Trojan War, the Trojan
Horse, the plundering of Ilios, and the winds which dispersed those
sailing from Troy, among them, Aeneas.

Tempting as it may be to establish an argument for a Dalmatian
Ilios squarely on the authority of classical authors, ultimately the
search for an understanding of Homeric geography in a Dalmatian
context must come from the supreme authority itself, the *Iliad's* own
evidence, and all references from classical sources must merely stand

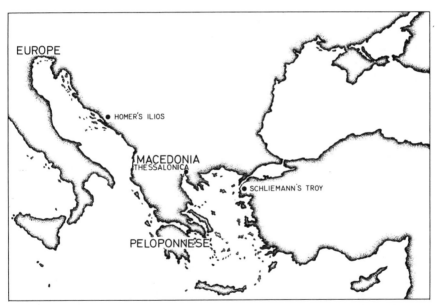

A scholium on Stephanos of Byzantium unequivocally places Ilios to
the west of Thessalonika, and not to the east, where popular tradition
locates it in Asia Minor. Many ancient writers were well aware of this
fact, but an explanation of their hints and allusions first requires a thorough understanding of a Homeric Ilios in a Dalmatian setting, and the
circumstances under which the would-be site of Homeric Ilios was
transferred to Asia Minor.

as corroboration of a particular author's knowledge of Homeric geography. The approach to answering the question of why Homeric Ilios was forsaken in favor of a bogus site at TROY VIII should not cloud the study of two separate issues: one is the study of Homeric geography in a Dalmatian context for whatever benefits it may yield; the other is the study of selecting those classical authors who were knowledgeable on questions of most ancient history.

But the parenthetic question arises; what, then, did Heinrich Schliemann uncover at Hissarlik? Evidently he uncovered the site that the Greeks themselves had identified, about 700 B.C., as the most plausible site for a Homeric Ilios, and that would best correspond with the Homeric account; before this time, Hissarlik had lain abandoned for four centuries—and what it had been, is an open question.

And then again, why did Greek colonists identify Hissarlik with the Homeric Ilios? The question, though not exactly a Homeric problem, deserves attention, yet it cannot be answered with certainty before running the gamut of putting the *Iliad* in its proper geographical context, and before understanding its *fundamental position as the point of departure for Greek history*; but, at the risk of revealing the conclusive argument of this book: it was a case of political chicanery.

PART II

CHAPTER 3

THE CORPUS OF
HOMERIC GEOGRAPHY

The corpus of Homeric geography is a tightly controlled structure of toponyms and ethnyms:

The nature and scope of the Homeric world is not so much a matter of speculating whether Homer was aware of all his facts or what the extent of his geographical knowledge was. It is a matter of understanding the *parameters of a geographical syntax in the language of a geographical grammar*; that is, the methodology of recording and classifying information of only what need be known, and at the same time describing peoples and places directly or indirectly associated with the Trojan War. In other words, there is nothing vague or factually mistaken in Homeric geography. The discipline was used with a hitherto unsuspected rigor. Sparse as Homeric geography may seem, the information extrapolated from its organization reaches encyclopaedic proportions.

Homeric geography, like grammar, is strictly formular, and therefore a system of classification is of medullar importance. The beginnings of clear Homeric thinking are in the proper divisions of things into orderly groups. The concept is applied most noticeably to geographical information, but it extends even to such aspects of the *Iliad* as the tailored character of the Trojan War participants—like automatons—according to their function.

The basic structure of the entire geographical corpus is divided into five well defined groups. Each group is again sub-divided into parts, which are again sub-divided into sub-parts. The five groups are in what may aptly be called a 'dactyl format' because, like the fingers of the hand, four groups are very much the same, while the fifth, not unlike the thumb is to the fingers, is altogether different. Thus, *all* of Homeric geography is contained in the following five groups:

1. CATALOGUE OF SHIPS

A listing, developed by the *Iliad's* authorship, structured in the dactyl format; the material is arranged to describe a neat schematic distribution of peoples and places up and down the length of the Italian peninsula, and across, with Dalmatia in the east and Sicily, Sardinia and Corsica in the west.

2. TROJAN FORCES (ABROAD)

A listing, developed by the *Iliad's* authorship, structured in eight parts (symbolic of the eight parts of speech), three of which correspond with the listing of local Trojan peoples and places (below), and the remaining five which describe a neat schematic distribution of peoples and places, of a Trojan allegiance, up and down the length of the Italian peninsula.

3. GROUP THREE

A listing (so called for want of a better name), assembled by the *Iliad's* reader, of peoples and places mentioned throughout the text that are neither listed in the *The Catalogue of Ships* nor *The Trojan Forces (Abroad)*, nor can they be strictly regarded as Trojans; the material is classified according to the following arrangement:

PHYSICAL GEOGRAPHY	SOCIAL GEOGRAPHY
mountains	districts
islands	tribes
rivers	towns
lakes	families

4. TROY

A listing, assembled by the *Iliad's* reader, of peoples and places mentioned in the *Catalogue of Ships*, the *Trojan Forces* and

elsewhere throughout the text, that are patently Trojan; the
material is classified according to the following arrangement:

PHYSICAL GEOGRAPHY	SOCIAL GEOGRAPHY
the sea	districts
islands	tribes
rivers	towns
mountains	places

5. ILIOS

The last is a group unlike the preceding two pairs. The nature
of the information is more on the topographical order rather
than geographical, in the strict sense of the word. It is a treatise,
so to speak, of all that can be gleaned from the text about the lay-
out and location of various buildings on Ilios, from which infer-
rences are to be made about their function as cult shrines.

Every single geonym (toponym or ethnym) within the five groups
may be thought of as a distinct 'element' with an intrinsic characteristic. In a sense, a geonym contains some sort of information, beginning
with what geographical type of word it is. This is followed by its meaning (where one can be ascertained), or by some tradition attached to it.
In some cases, when accompanied by an epithet, it begs for an identification somewhere within the area of its geographical context. A
geonym may be likened to a piece from a jig-saw puzzle: it's position
within the whole is determined by its shape and its color.

Take the word *Satnioeïs*, as an example (*Iliad*, translated by A. T.
Murray, The Loeb Classical Library, 1960; all subsequent quotes from
the *Iliad* are taken from this translation and shown in italics):

> . . . and the king of men, Agamemnon, slew Elatos that dwelt in
> steep Pedasos by the banks of fair-flowing Satnioeïs.
>
> VI, 34

Obviously *Satnioeïs* does not correspond with the *Catalogue of Ships*
nor the *Trojan Forces* nor *Ilios*, since it does not appear in these groups.
Therefore, it belongs with either *Group Three*, the geonyms which are
to be identified somewhere along the length and breadth of Italy, or
with *Troy*, somewhere along the coast of Dalmatia.

Now, *Satnioeïs* is mentioned again:

*"-Altes that is lord over the war-loving Leleges, holding steep
Pedasos on the Satnioeïs."*

XXI, 87

and the jig-saw puzzle piece begins to fall in place from the following:

*"Not now for the first time shall I stand forth against swift-
footed Achilles; nay, once ere now he drave me with his spear
from Ida, when he had come forth against our kine, and laid
Lyrnessos waste and Pedasos withal; howbeit Zeus saved me
. . . Else had I been slain beneath the hands of Achilles and
of Athene, who ever went before him and set there a light of
deliverance, and bade him slay Leleges and Trojans with spear
of bronze."*

XX, 89

This shows that *Satnioeïs* must be classified with the *Troy* group, for
the anecdote about Achilles' raid corresponds with the plundering of
the Trojan coast in the days prior to the *Iliad's* opening.[1]

Of the eight possible geonym classifications available for the *Troy*
group, the name of *Satnioeïs* must fall to that of Rivers, as suggested by:

. . . Pedasos by the banks of fair-flowing Satnioeïs . . .

loc. cit.

And since it is not likely to be one of Scamander's tributaries, (for the
anecdote about Aeneas is that of a coastal raid), one will search in vain
in an atlas for other rivers in the Dalmatian coast: none exists south of
the Neretva, yet to the north, the Cetina is a good choice because of a
desired proximity with the Scamander's delta-valley (mentioned in the
story of Achilles' coastal raids), and because of the phonetic similarity
between *satni-* and *cetin-*.

That the *Satnioeïs* should be identified with the Cetina, regardless of
any questionable validity in the phonetic similarity of the Homeric
with the modern name, is implied in a roundabout way in the identification of 'steep Pedasos' with Omiš at the mouth of the Cetina, of which
Fodor's Modern Guides, YUGOSLAVIA 1964, (David McKay Co., Inc.,
N.Y., 1964) says the following (p. 181):

---

1. The story about the towns Achilles raided prior to the *Iliad's* openning (recorded in
Apollodorus, *The Epitome*) has come to us from non-Homeric sources. Two views may be
assumed about its origins: one, that it was partially recorded in the *Iliad* but that a fuller
account came to us through an independent source; the other, that the story came to us as
a knowledgeable comment on the *Iliad's* lines '"seven well-peopled cities . . ."' from one
who understood their meaning in their proper geographical context.

The road south from Split leads through the fishing village of Omiš, at the mouth of the River Catine [*sic*]. Once a pirate hide-out, the bay is hidden between cliffs rising steeply to a height of nearly 1,000 feet, presided over by an old fortress. There is an excellent, gently sloping sand beach . . .

It now becomes apparent what sort of a terrible man Agamemnon was, when he offered Achilles:

> . . . *"seven well-peopled cities . . . Cardamyle, Enope, and grassy Hire and sacred Pherae and Antheia with deep meadows and fair Aepeia and vine-clad Pedasos. All are nigh to the sea on the nethermost borders of sandy Pylos."*

IX, 149

These towns are not to be found in the Gulf of Messenia (where vestiges of ruins are wanting for some of them); instead, they are:

> *". . . nigh to the sea on the nethermost borders . . ."*

ibid.

of the long and narrow V-shaped Stonski Bay (the *pýlos* enclosed between the northern shores of the Pelješac peninsula and the mainland), which the very Achilles himself had sacked!

So much for Satnioeïs, though one wonders about the 'war-loving Leleges,' and the Illyrians' later reputation as pirates.[2]

The revelation in reading the *Iliad's* narration and the body of its geographical information in a different context is extraordinary. Indeed, the proposition almost seems to rub the wrong way: all the concomitant historical associations attached to a geonym—which is a wealth of myth in need of re-interpretation—and a number of other important considerations, such as those pertaining to language or to cult-rites, must be understood in a different light, as in a Doppler shift, moving from one end of the spectrum to the other.

But, however difficult or strange it may seem to regard the pre-Homeric Greek heritage (or expedient to accept the status quo), one basic question must beg the issue: can *rational* sense be made of the *Iliad* in an Asia Minor context?

The reader will judge for himself.

---

2. The Illyrians were an early pre-Trojan people who were said to have been descended from Illyrus, son of Cadmus. In historical times they were known as fierce pirates who found protection in the cover of Dalmatia's highly indented coastline.

CHAPTER 4

EIGHT
GEOGRAPHICAL COMPARISONS

There follows below a demonstration, on a comparative basis, of eight instances which show that the *Iliad's* geographical prerequisites for the site of Ilios are:

1. Incompatible with the site of Hissarlik and
2. suit a setting in a Dalmatian context.

I have chosen the easiest instance from each of the eight classifications into which the geonyms of the group *4. Troy* fall. They are a sufficient representation of the entire physical and social spectrum of Trojan geography, as to go through the text and lift a greater number of other instances cannot serve any greater practical purpose.

1. THE SEA

There is a reference to a non-existent sea in the east of Asia Minor, when:

> *The sun was now just striking on the fields, as he arose from soft-gliding, deep-flowing Oceanos . . .*

> VII, 422

and another, when:

> *Now Eos the saffron-robed arose from the streams of Oceanos to bring light to immortals and to mortal men . . .*

> XIX, 1

But the sun can only rise from the Propontis, or beyond, from the Euxine, at its greatest northern declination during summer days with an azimuth of 58°28'. Or it can rise from the eastern shores of the Gulf of Adramytium, or beyond, from the Mediterranean environs of Cyprus, at its greatest southern declination during winter days with an azimuth of 121°33'. Otherwise, the sun cannot rise from the sea.

Since it cannot be determined, in the instances mentioned above, whether the sun is rising during summer or winter days, the idea of a sea in the east of Asia Minor must be strengthened by making Oceanos circuitous by nature, as around the embossed allegorical scenes on the Shield of Achilles:

> *Therein he set also the great might of the river Oceanos,*
> *around the uttermost rim of the strongly wrought shield.*

XVIII, 607

And indeed, the nature of Oceanos must be circuitous, and there must be a sea in the east of Asia Minor, or else:

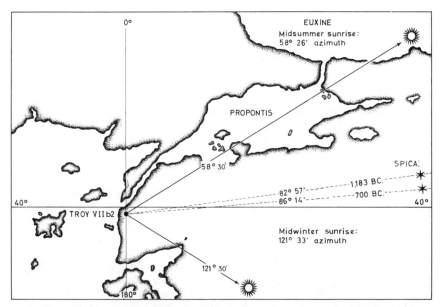

In Asia Minor, the sun rises from the sea only during the solstices, but Spica cannot ever have risen from the sea (unless the intended sense is that it will have done so by having set in it many hours previously).

> *. . . the star of harvest-time that shineth bright above all others*
> *when he hath bathed him in the stream of Oceanos . . .*
>
> V, 6

cannot be so.
  Furthermore:

> *. . . the star of harvest-time that shineth bright above all others . . .*
>
> ibid.

is to be identified with Spica, a prominent 1.21 magnitude star (not
Sirius, that would shine bright*est* above all others), which will have
had, in 1,200 B.C., a declination on the celestial sphere of +5°29′, and
risen with an azimuth of 82°50′, and in 700 B.C. (when Hissarlik was
again occupied, this time by Aeolian colonists), a declination of +2°52′,
and risen with an azimuth of 86°14′. In neither instance will Spica
have been anywhere near a sea.[1]
  Now, the idea of a sea in the east of Asia Minor, aided by that of the
circuitous sense of Oceanos, must be false, for Homer cannot be invent-
ing a non-existent geography, nor giving a factual account of what cannot be verified,[2] and so the argument at once becomes moot.

  In the geographical context of a Dalmatian setting, the intended sea
to the east of Troy is the Euxine; the sun rises from the sea throughout
the year, with the exception of the days between the beginning of May
and the end of July, when its northerly declination in a general northeastern direction is placed beyond the Euxine's northern shores. And
Spica, in 1,183 B.C. (if this date for the Trojan War is credible) will
have risen with an azimuth of 82°50′ in the general area of the
Euxine's northern waters. Still, a later date for reporting this event
(and I would favour about 1,000 B.C. for the composition of the *Iliad*)
would place the rising of Spica some degrees further south (clear-
ing the southern tip of the Tauric Chersonesos) and so making the
statement:

> *. . . when he hath bathed him in the stream of Oceanos . . .*
>
> loc. cit.

a perfectly sound affirmation.

---

1. I am indebted to Ing. Guillermo Mallén Fullerton, former president of the Sociedad
Astronomica de Mexico, for his assistance with these and all subsequent statements on
positional astronomy.
2. Of course, an argument could be made in favour of a sea in the East of Asia Minor by
making the Caspian, which is salt, the intended sea; but such an argument would seem
to lead nowhere.

The river-like sense of:

> ... *soft-gliding, deep-flowing Oceanos* ...
>
> VII, 422
>
> ... *the great might of the river Oceanos* ...
>
> XVIII, 607
>
> ... *the stream of Oceanos* ...
>
> XIX, 1

is lent by the swift and dangerous currents through the Bosphorus and the Dardanelles which connect the Euxine with the Aegean.

But the circuitous nature of Oceanos, adduced from the statement:

> ... *around the uttermost rim of the strongly wrought shield* ...
>
> loc. cit.

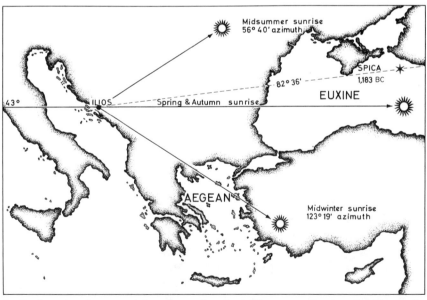

In Dalmatia, the sun rising from the river-like sea refers to the Euxine's connection with the Aegean through the Propontis. Spica will have risen from the Euxine, thus eliminating the need of suggesting it will have risen from the sea by having set in it many hours previously.

as if it were a stream circumscribing the known and unknown bounds of the earth, and coming back upon itself, would appear to require a connection between the Euxine and the Adriatic headwaters. Yet this proposition is so naïve as to be absurd, for Homer could easily have verified whether or not any such connection through the northern Balkans existed, and must be rejected at once in favor of another rationalization: it is not difficult to suppose that Homer conceived of the world as a sphere on which an irregular line representing the shore-line (both the already known and the presupposed) came back upon itself[3] (not unlike the curved line on a tennis ball which divides it into irregular hemispheres, as if one representing the sea, and the other land), and that this line had some portion of it indented in such a way as to represent the Mediterranean and its adjoining seas.

2. ISLANDS

The alignment of islands in the Aegean required for a scene of Zeus and Poseidon, who become metamorphosically fused into a gleaming, golden sunset reflecting a shimmering beam of light off the surface of the sea, is impossible. To wit:

> Now Zeus . . . turned away his bright eyes, and looked afar, upon the land of the Thracian horsemen . . . To Troy he no longer in any wise turned his bright eyes . . .
>
> But the lord, the Shaker of Earth, kept no blind watch, for he sat marvelling at the war and the battle, high on the topmost peak of wooded Samothrace, for from thence all Ida was plain to see; and plain to see were the city of Priam, and the ships of the Achaeans . . .
>
> Forthwith then he went down from the rugged mount, striding forth with swift footsteps . . . Thrice he strode in his course, and with the fourth stride he reached his goal, even Aegae, where was his famous palace builded in the depths of the mere, golden and gleaming, imperishable forever. Thither came he, and let harness beneath his car his two bronze-hooved horses . . .
>
> There is a wide cavern in the depths of the deep mere, midway between Tenedos and rugged Imbros. There Poseidon, the Shaker of Earth, stayed his horses, and loosed them from the

---

3. In fact, that this line should *not* come back upon itself poses some rather interesting problems on the order of Moëbius-like solids.

*car, and cast before them food ambrosial to graze upon . . . and
himself he went to the host of the Achaeans.*

XIII, 1 et pas.

As the day is done, Zeus and Poseidon are both:

. . . high on the topmost peak of wooded Samothrace . . .

ibid.

and Zeus, in the personification of the day, (as Apollo is of the sun),
instead of looking in a westerly direction of a sunset, looks in the
northeastern direction of a summer sunrise:

. . . upon the land of the Thracian horsemen . . .

ibid.

He is headed, so to speak, for the following day's sunrise and, as quaint
geography goes, this is acceptable (though the presence of Poseidon
requires some pondering).

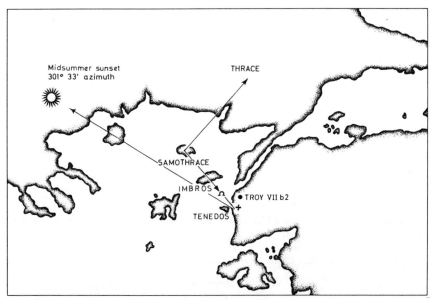

**In Asia Minor, the sun's greatest northern declination at a Midsummer
sunset in the environs of Hissarlik is 301° 33', and the required align-
ments of Samothrace and Imbros with a supposed grotto between Imbros and Tenedos for a sunset is beyond the sun's greatest possible
declination.**

But the initial problem, before compounding, lies in the name of
Samothrace which, though the text specifically reads:

> . . . *high on the topmost peak of Samos wooded-Thracelike . . .*
>
> XIII, 12

is erroneously accepted as:

> . . . *high on the topmost peak of wooded Samothrace . . .*

Consequently the question about 'the topmost peak of Samos,' which is
an island far away to the south, is a puzzle. And so be it, but for the
sake of argument, let us assume it is Samothrace, and not Samos, that
is intended.[4]

So, when Poseidon, left the peak of Samothrace:

> . . . *Thrice he strode in his course, and with the fourth stride he
> reached his goal, even Aegae, where was his famous palace
> builded in the depths of the mere . . .*
>
> ibid.

The sense is that he strode from the island of Samothrace itself, onto
the sea, then to the island of Imbros, and again to the sea in the environs of Tenedos (or the tiny island of Mavros just north of Tenedos),
since Aegae is:

> . . . *a wide cavern in the depths of the deep mere, midway
> between Tenedos and rugged Imbros.*
>
> ibid.

Yet there exists no such cavern, nor shoals of any sort which might
possibly be thought of as a cavern.

The final objection to the setting of this scene in the Aegean is that
the alignment of Samothrace, Imbros and Tenedos is only possible in
an area a considerable distance to the south of Hissarlik, and that this
alignment is well beyond the sun's greatest northern declination of a
midsummer sunset with an azimuth of 301°33'.

In the geographical context of a Dalmatian setting

> . . . *the topmost peak of Samos wooded-Thracelike . . .*
>
> loc. cit.

---

4. It was explained, in ancient times, that the original name of Samothrace was once
Samos, and so, the rendering of . . . *Samos wooded-Thracelike* . . . , in an Asia Minor
context, makes Homer use the same name for two different places.

is to be identified with the 3,153-foot heights of Sveti Jlija on the western tip of the Pelješac peninsula. The peak is very nearly on the 43rd parallel—just south of it, within a few seconds of an arc—so, when Zeus:

> . . . *looked afar, upon the land of the Thracian horsemen . . .*
>
> loc. cit.

he did so in a straight line (along the 43rd parallel), across the Adriatic, into Italy, over Monte Cavallo (Horse Mountain), and the land of the Thracians,[5] (whose name has survived in that of Lake Trasimeno).

So, Poseidon:

> *Forthwith then he went down from the rugged mount . . . Thrice he strode in his course . . .*
>
> loc. cit.

initiating his strides with the right foot on the peak of Samos, as it were, and stepped as if on stepping-stones: *first*, with the left foot on the northwest tip of Korčula (the northernmost point), *second*, with the right foot on the southwest tip of Viš (the southernmost point), and *third*, with the left foot on the north tip of Biševo (the northern most point). As seen from the heights of Samos, the sun, only on this particular evening of an equinox, sets on the horizon and reflects a path of gold (the metamorphosical fusion of Zeus and Poseidon) which appears to be just wide enough to embrace the tips of the islands that resemble markers on either side of an avenue of light.

At the end of the northernmost point of Biševo is the cove of Balun, which is precisely where Poseidon:

> . . . *with the fourth stride he reached his goal, even Aegae, where was his famous palace builded in the depths of the mere, golden and gleaming, imperishable forever.*
>
> loc. cit.

Concerning this cove, the Yugoslav Lexicographical Institute's *THE YUGOSLAV COAST Guide Book and Atlas*, (Zagreb, 1966), under BIŠEVO (p.5), says the following:

---

5. That the Thracians can be identified with a people in the environs of Lake Trasimeno suggests, conversely, that Samos is to be found on the same parallel, to the east; furthermore, such a west-east association of Thrace-Samos suggests a connection with the Samothracian Mysteries, which in turn invites further speculation that the lengthy description of a sunset is an Orphic commemoration of a Spring or Autumnal Equinox. For more on the Thracians, see below, 4. MOUNTAINS and 6. TRIBES.

The caves by the sea include the famous Blue Cave (Modra Spilja) in the cove of Balun. At noon, when the sea is calm, sunrays penetrating into the Blue Cave through a hole under the surface are reflected from the white bottom, and illuminate the cave with a blue, and the objects in the water with a silver light. The beauty of this cave, which was made accessible in 1848, makes it a great attraction . . .

But alas!

Thither came he . . .

loc. cit.

yet, the location of:

. . . a wide cavern in the depths of the deep mere, midway between Tenedos and rugged Imbros.

loc. cit.

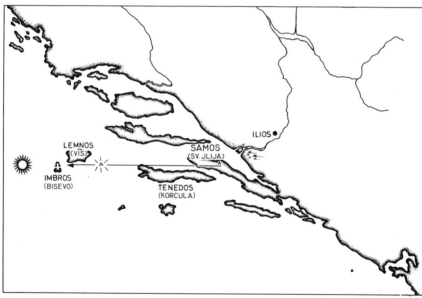

In Dalmatia, the exact east-west alignment of a sunset as seen from the summit of Samos (Sveti Ilija) with outward lying islands denotes a Spring or Autumn equinox. The grotto of Aegae is to be identified with Modra Spilja (Magician's Cave) on Biševo, and the illusion of a sunset between Imbros (Biševo) and Tenedos (Korčula) is explained by the illusion of the sun's theoretical position the instant after sunset.

at once becomes a conflicting statement, for *messegýs*, 'midway between' Tenedos and Imbros is not at the cove of Balun. This suggests
that either the text has been tampered with to more or less accommodate it to an Asia Minor setting, or that the problem must be ratio-
nalized in some other way, for the sequence in the notion of a sunset
has not yet come to an end. The second alternative is the better one:
messegýs is one of those marvellous Homeric words which lend themselves to elasticity of interpretation; it puns with *sekós*, 'a pen, fold,' as
indeed Aegae is, and elicits its aptness for the C-shaped contour of
Balun, so that *mésson sékos*, 'a middle pen,' must then actually be a
place between Tenedos and Imbros.

The explanation for the puzzling site of this place is the following:
the instant the lower rim of the the sun's disk touches the horizon, it is
behind Imbros (Biševo), and the island, being nearer the observer than
the horizon, appears slightly below it. Therefore, the instant the upper
rim of the sun's disk sinks below the horizon and disappears into the
cove of Balun, the lower rim is that much further below (in the propor-
tion of the sun's diameter), and consequently, as an optical illusion,
that much nearer the observer than Imbros itself. As seen from the
summit of Samos, the theoretical position for the sun's disk, with reference to the horizon, is a place *exactly*:

> . . . *midway between Tenedos and rugged Imbros* . . .
>
> loc. cit.

3. RIVERS

The existing river systems in Asia Minor are altogether inadequate for
meeting the prerequisites of a river swollen with the torrential waters
from its tributaries, as in the following:

> . . . *verily did Poseidon and Apollo take counsel to sweep away
> the wall, bringing against it the might of all the rivers that flow
> forth from the mountains of Ida to the sea—Rhesos and
> Heptaporos and Caresos and Rhodios, and Granicus and
> Aesepos, and goodly Scamander, and Simoïs, by the banks
> whereof many shields of bull's-hide and many helms fell in the
> dust . . . of all these did Phoebus Apollo turn the mouths
> together, and for nine days' space he drave their flood against
> the wall* . . .
>
> XII, 17

The Menderes, which is identified with the Scamander, has tributaries scarcely amounting to more than creeks. Furthermore, if one
looks in a classical atlas, the Granicus and the Aesepos (which to judge
from the text are tributaries of the Scamander) are made to debouch
into the Propontis, thus making it difficult to understand how their
waters, with those of other tributaries, were able to contribute towards
a flood.[6] Of course, the inference to be drawn is that some tidal wave
from the sea? or perhaps a storm? of devastating proportions simply
swept away the Danaans' defensive wall. It has even been suggested
this incident reflects a local memory of the horrible consequences from
the volcanic explosion of Thera in earlier times.

---

6. Presumably, when the Scamander became identified with the Menderes, it was impossible to name its creeks after the list of tributaries that Homer gave—for they simply
could not qualify as rivers—and so the nearest rivers of the vicinity were named after
Scamander's tributaries, regardless of the implications in the Homeric statement about a
flood—which, after all, was only 'narrative poetry.'

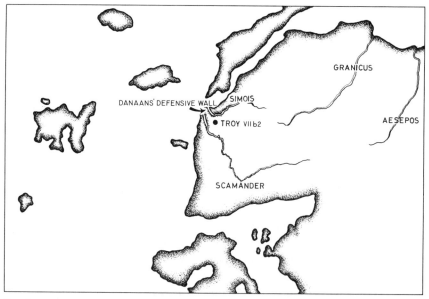

In Asia Minor, the Scamander has a sparse tributary system barely
amounting to rivulets. Consequently, those tributaries whose torrential
floods swept away the Danaans' defensive wall beg to be identified as
rivers, even if they debouch elsewhere and suggest the interpretation of
a tidal wave.

But there is still another objection: the Simoïs, which is identified
with the Dumbrek, is made to flow into the Scamander. To wit:

> But when they were come to the land of Troy and the two flowing
> rivers, where Simoïs and Scamander join their streams . . .
>
> V, 774

The Dumbrek does not, nor was it ever likely to have run into the
Menderes. It is so impeded by the terrain's natural contours, that it
must turn from its westward flow and run a course parallel with the
final portion of the Menderes to debouch east of it. Were the Dumbrek
not so impeded, it would have joined the Menderes and not debouch
where it does. However, the point could be labored that the Menderes
and the Dumbrek do join their waters, at the sea; or that the mouths of
each are to be brought back to a common estuary; or even that the
Dumbrek is in fact joined to the Menderes via a canal, and so on.[7]

---

7. This problem of where it is the Simoïs and the Scamander meet, distorts an understanding of where it is that Hera came to Troy and stayed her horses, for which argument, see 8. PLACES.

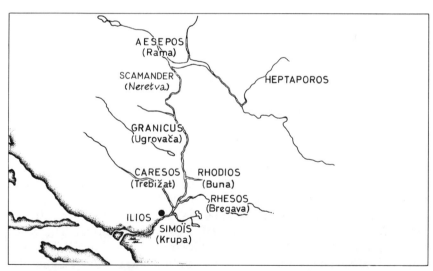

In Dalmatia, the Neretva, identified with the Scamander, collects such
vast quantities of water from its tributaries that torrential floods have
been known, within recent times, to wreak havoc in its delta-valley.
Each of their Homeric names denotes a geological peculiarity.

In the geographical context of a Dalmatian setting, the Scamander is
to be identified with the Neretva, which rises high in the hinterland
mountains, and is met in its course to the sea by several important
tributaries. It flows through a marshy plain before debouching, and it
is indeed possible that:

> *. . . the might of all the rivers that flow forth from the mountains
> of Ida to the sea . . . of all these did Phoebus Apollo turn the
> mouths together . . . and drave their flood against the wall . . .*
>   loc. cit.

It is on record that floods have wreaked havoc in the delta-valley, so
much so, that ever since prehistoric times, towns have settled on the
safety of higher ground in the surrounding hillsides. Today, the final
portions of the Neretva have been embanked to insure an orderly flow
to the sea.

The sequential order in the listing of tributaries is in a schematic
order, according to their nature and their location, thus:

RHESOS:	Bregava
HEPTAPOROS:	
CARESOS:	Trebižat
RHODIOS:	Buna
GRANICOS:	Ugrovača
AESEPOS:	Rama
SCAMANDER:	Neretva
SIMOIS:	Krupa

HEPTAPOROS and SCAMANDER. The Scamander's watershed rises,
in a sense, at the sources of its tributaries, which are several: of the two
uppermost in the hinterland, likened to a letter **Y**, of which one arm is
also the body of the stem, one must be the Scamander itself (the stretch
which is the main geological channel of the river's course). The other
arm must then be the Heptaporos, whose name 'seven fords' (but perhaps better 'seven openings,' as in the English sense of the *passage* of a
pore), and its schematic relationship with Scamander suggests, should
be located a sufficient distance up-stream for its waters to pass by the
mouths of *seven* tributaries.

AESEPOS and SIMOIS. The identity of the Simoïs, which means 'snub-nosed,' with the Krupa, which drains two lakes on the left bank of the Neretva's delta-marshes, is inferred from its location near Ilios, when Ares called:

> . . . to the Trojans from the topmost citadel, and now again as he sped by the shores of Simoïs over Callicolone.

> XX, 53

and therefore explains why Scamander:

> . . . called with a shout to Simoïs: "Dear brother . . . fill thy streams with water from thy springs . . ."

> XXI, 307

The identity of the Aesepos, meaning 'ever marshy,' with the Rama, which also drains two lakes in the upper reaches of the Neretva, where

> . . . they that dwelt in Zeleia . . . that drink the dark water of Aesepos . . .

> II, 824

is inferred from the similar setting of the Rama's valley district (now damed) with the delta-marshes about Ilios, and so called because the district *emulated* or *resembled* the environs of Ilios.

RHESOS and CARESOS. These two names have the root *rhéo*, 'to flow' in common. Since the Caresos means 'flowing hair,' it is easily identified with the Trebižat because of the beautiful hair-like cascades at its confluence with the Neretva. Opposite is the Rhesos, which means 'the flowing one,' to be identified with the Bregava, simply because of all the Neretva's tributaries, it is the one which carries the greatest amount of water.

RHODIOS and GRANICOS. These share a color, as if the *rose* redness of Rhodios were somehow associated with a *granate* redness of Granicos. Since the name of Rhodios is akin with *rhóthion*, 'a dashing wave: surge,' 'a loud roar,' it may be identified with the Buna, which, though a very short tributary, wells up from the depths of the earth with a thundering roar. The name of Granicos is akin to *kranaós*, 'rugged, rocky, stony', and may be identified with the Ugrovača which never meets the Neretva; instead, by the same token the Rhodios *emerges* from the earth, it *disappears* into the stony and porous ground.

4. MOUNTAINS

The 5,796-foot mountain to the southeast of Hissarlik identified as Ida, the summit of which is called Gargaros, is wanting in adequate geographical location to suit the scene of a moonset casting a reflection off the surface of the sea, as it does not align correctly for Hera's voyage from Thrace, via Athos, to Gargaros. Witness her impossible zig-zag course over the sea, when:

> ... *Hera darted down and left the peak of Olympos; on Pieria she stepped and lovely Emathia, and sped over the snowy mountains of the Thracian horsemen, even over their top-most peaks ... and from Athos she stepped upon the billowy sea, and so came to Lemnos, the city of godlike Thoas ...*
>
> *But when she had sworn and made an end of the oath, the twain left the cities of Lemnos and Imbros ... To many-fountained Ida they came ... even to Lecton, where first they left the sea; and the twain fared on over the dry land ...*

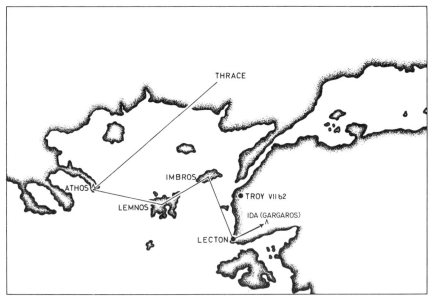

In Asia Minor, an allusion to the apparent lunar retrocession from west to east in Hera's voyage from Thrace to Gargaros traces an impossible zig-zag course.

> *But Hera swiftly drew nigh to topmost Gargaros, the peak of*
> *lofty Ida, and Zeus, the cloud-gatherer, beheld her.*
> XIV, 225 et pas.

But Hera's voyage across the sea, rather than being the description of a moonset dipping below the horizon within the space of a few hours is, in fact, a scene of the moon's apparent retrocession, slipping back upon its orbit, and gaining on itself from west to east.[8] Not only is the required alignment wanting, but so are the topological characteristics for the summit of Ida, for it is neither throat-like or gargoylesque, nor in any way similar to the cone or crater of a volcano, such as to warrant the name of:

> *. . . Gargaros, the peak of lofty Ida . . .*
> ibid.

In the geographical context of a Dalmatian setting, the course of Hera's fortnight-voyage from west to east begins over the Italian peninsula, and:

> *. . . from Athos she stepped upon the billowy sea . . .*
> loc. cit.

which is to be identified with Pedaso, on the Adriatic coast, just south of where the Aso river debouches,

> *. . . and so came to Lemnos . . .*
> loc. cit.

the island which is contiguous with Imbros, and to be identified with Viš.

Lemnos and Imbros align exactly with the eastern tip of the island of Hvar and a gorge in the high-rising Biokovo range on the mainland. So, after Hera's sojourn on Lemnos (and this is the period of time that suggests the two-week lunar retrocession from west to east[9]):

---

8. After the 15th day of its cycle, so that in the late-afternoon-early-evening of the 28th or 29th day, it appears almost full above the eastern horizon.

I have reckoned the lunar cycle to begin with a Full Moon rising over the eastern horizon on the evening of the 30th day of its previous cycle which is the 1st day of its new cycle, and a New Moon setting on the western horizon on the evening of the 15th day, rather than the conventional New Moon starting off the cycle with a Full Moon on the 15th day.

9. This instance of Hera, moving from west to east, clearly shows an added dimension to the *Iliad* (when studied in its correct geographical context) as a strictly cyclical account of the events of a Trojan War, from which are adduced a pre-conceived structure for an account, and the ritual aspect of the events narrated.

> *. . . the twain* [Hera and Hypnos, the light and dark halves of
> the 3rd quarter moon] *left the cities of Lemnos and Imbros . . .*
>
> loc. cit.

and gaining on its orbit:

> *. . . To many fountained Ida they came . . .*
>
> loc. cit.

but, before arriving, came:

> *. . . even to Lecton, where first they left the sea . . .*
>
> loc. cit.

which must be the island of Hvar, rather than the name of a place on
the mainland, since a gloss of the text for Trojan names does not show
any other than 'Lecton' for that of an island.

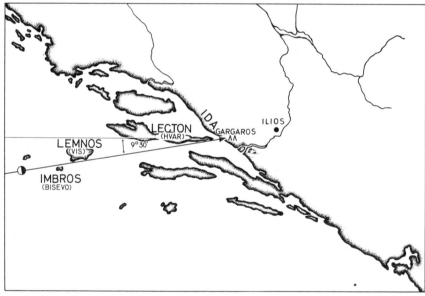

In Dalmatia, Imbros (Biševo) and Lemnos (Viš) are aligned with the
eastern tip of Lecton (Hvar) and the crags of Gargaros. The text's
sequence in 'the twin cities of Lemnos and Imbros . . .' suggest it has
been altered to suit Asia Minor, and this only reference to Lecton 'where
first she [Hera] left the sea . . .' supplies the name for this island (that
would otherwise remain innominate) rather than that of a place on the
mainland from where to leave the sea.

Thence:

> . . . *the twain fared on over the dry land* . . .
> *But Hera swiftly drew nigh to topmost Gargaros, the peak of*
> *lofty Ida* . . .

loc. cit.

the name of which is answered by the funnel-like gorge of towering
2,526- and 3,008-foot crags, as if the reduplication *gar-gar* suggested a
throat (cf. Spanish *gárgara*, 'gargle').

But there is a difference in the angle of alignment between the initial course of retrocession from Athos to Lemnos (which to all intents
and purposes is exactly due west) and the subsequent course, from
Lemnos and Imbros to Lecton and Gargaros, which is deflected by almost 10°. There is, in a sense, a zig-zag in the course of retrocession
over a period of 15 days, but this variation in the alignment is accounted for by the fact the moon swings widely from one position to
another (at moonrise or moonset) in the course of one lunation. It is
therefore in keeping that if a moonset was observed at 270° on the 15th
day of the lunar cycle, the alignment of a moonrise on the 30th day
should have shifted by 10°.

5. DISTRICTS

The Troic (a better translation than Trojan) Plain was obviously in the
general area between the Danaans' defensive wall at the Hellespont,
and the site of Hissarlik further inland. It is mentioned by name only
twice, once when Agamemnon:

> *So often as he gazed toward the Troic Plain, he marvelled at the*
> *many fires that burned before the face of Ilios* . . . *but when-*
> *soever he looked toward the ships and the host of the Achaeans,*
> *then many were the hairs that he pulled from his head* . . .

X, 11

and once again, when Idomeneus looked into the distance:

> . . . *But the Argives sitting in the place of gathering were gazing*
> *at the horses, that flew amid the dust over the plain* . . . "*but now*
> *can I nowhere spy them, though mine eyes glance everywhither*
> *over the Troic Plain, as I gaze* . . ."

XXIII, 448 et pas.

The location of the Troic Plain between the enemy's encampment and the site of Ilios is pretty well established from the above instances. Therefore the location of the Ileian Plain, mentioned only once, when Agenor was chased by Achilles:

> *"But what if I leave . . . and with my feet flee from the wall elsewhither, toward the Ileian Plain, until I be come to the glens and spurs of Ida? . . . Then at even, when I have bathed me in the river and cooled me of my sweat, I might get me back to Ilios."*

XXI, 558

will have been in the country to the south of Hissarlik, up-stream the Menderes, near Ida.

But the locations of these plains are subject to the positive identification of Ilios with the site of Hissarlik, and will not have held up during the times when scholars seemed certain that Ilios was to be identified

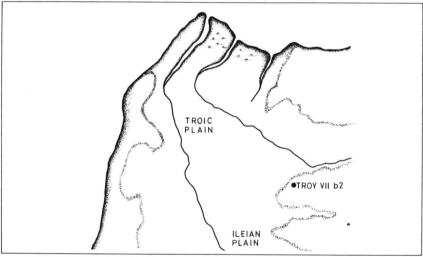

In Asia Minor, the Troic Plain is between the Danaans' camp beside the Hellespont shores and TROY VIIb2, and the Ileian Plain is therefore to be identified with the countryside further south, towards the peaks of Ida. Why these districts were so called (and distinguished from that of Dardania) can only be answered with educated guesses.

with the site of Bally Dag, near the Bunarbashi springs, south of the currently accepted location of the Ileian Plain.

Furthermore, though the identification of Ilios with Hissarlik has helped in the definition of parameters for the identification of certain topological feature, there remains the puzzle of why the Troic and Ileian Plains were so called, and why not the other way about. Even more, there is no satisfactory explanation of how these plains are to be distinguished from the district called Dardania.[10]

In the geographical context of a Dalmatian setting, the location of the enemy encampment will have been any place offering the best strategic advantage along the Neretva's right bank, from the confluence of the Norino downstream to the sea. The Troic Plain is then to be identified with the Glibuša marshes interposed between this place and the

---

10. For which, see the following chapter.

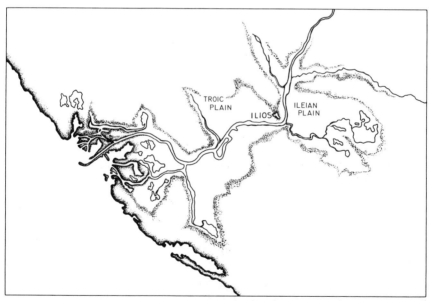

In Dalmatia, the marshes of the Troic Plain are so called on a pun of *drósos*, 'dew' with Tros, after whom Troy was named, as the topological counterpart to the marshes of the Ileian Plain, separated by a spit, itself so called on a pun of *i-lâas*, 'long stone' with Ilos, after whom Ilios was named.

site of Gabela. Since the name Troic does not seem to have a topological association with *trógo*, 'gnaw,' 'chew,' 'cut,' the marshes are then aptly named on a pun with *dríos*, 'thicket, brushwood' because of the dense vegetation of bullrushes and thickets, or, on a pun with *drósos*, 'dew,' 'pure water,' because of their crystalline waters.[11]

The Ileian Plain is to be identified with the Hutovo marshes situated opposite the Glibuša marshes. These are almost divided in half by the long and narrow Ostrovo limestone spit, and both halves are drained by the Krupa river. Though the name Troic might seem apt for this plain, because of the sense of 'cut,' it must be discarded in favor of Ileian (and not Ilian), which suggests an allusion to the *long*ness of the spit, and so its name would seem to be derived from an intensive inseparable prefix *i* + *lâas*, 'stone.' Hence, Agenor considered:

> "... *with my feet flee from the wall* [of Ilios] *elsewhither, toward the Ileian Plain, until I be come to the glens and spurs of Ida?*

loc. cit.

And:

> ... *at even, when I have bathed me in the river and cooled me of my sweat, I might get me back to Ilios."*

loc. cit.

6. TRIBES

Of the various Trojan allies, the Mysoi are mentioned in the listing of the *Trojan Forces*:

> ... *and of the Mysoi the Captains were Chromis and Ennomos the augur* ...

II, 858

And again, elsewhere:

> ... *the strong-hooved mules that toil in harness, which on a time the Mysoi had given to Priam, a splendid gift.*

XXIV, 278

---

11. That is, the nation Troy (properly Troia) was so called because of its *division* into *three* parts, but the Trojan (properly Troic) Plain, was so called on a pun with *dríos*, 'thicket,' and *drósos*, 'dew.'

Now, any classical atlas makes the country of Mysia out of the Mysoi people, and shows it in the Troad's southeastern hinterland. Yet Mysia, as a country, is not given in the text, as is, for instance, the country of Thrace of the Thracian people. Mysia, then, is an invention, as the Mysoi are explicitly placed as neighbors of the Thracians, when:

> *Now Zeus . . . turned away his bright eyes, and looked afar,*
> *upon the land of the Thracian horsemen, and of the Mysoi that*
> *fight in close combat, and of the lordly Hippemolgoi that drink*
> *the milk of mares, and of the Abioi, the most righteous of men.*
> XIII, 1

No wonder, the puzzling question mark in the *Index to Proper Names* of the Loeb Classical Library's *Iliad*, listing the Mysoi thus:

Mysoí, in Asia, ii. 858; x. 430; xiv. 512; xxiv. 278
Mysoí, in Europe (?), xiii. 5

In Asia Minor, Mysia is the hinterland country southeast of Troy, and the name is likelier derived from Mizraim, a biblical people mentioned in *Genesis*, rather than being an unwarranted fabrication of Mysia from Mysians (following the instance of Thrace from Thracians), a people specifically mentioned as neighbors of the Thracians who lived in the direction of a sunset.

The explanation, that at some early date a colony of Mysoi from Asia
Minor moved into Thracian territory, and so attracted sufficient attention to be recorded as neighbors of Thracians, does not ring the right
way: it is impossible to infer the location of the Mysoi in Asia Minor
from the instances in which they are mentioned in the text, and in
direct contradiction to the factual statement about their contiguity
with the Thracians.

In the geographical context of a Dalmatian setting, the connection of
the name Thrace with that of Lake Trasimeno in central Italy, and the
association of Thracian horsemen with the name of Monte Cavallo
(Horse Mountain) southeast of Assisi, is established by the scene of a
sunset along the 43rd parallel, when Zeus:

> . . . turned away his bright eyes, and looked afar, upon the land
> of the Thracian horsemen, and of the Mysoi that fight in close
> combat . . .

loc. cit.

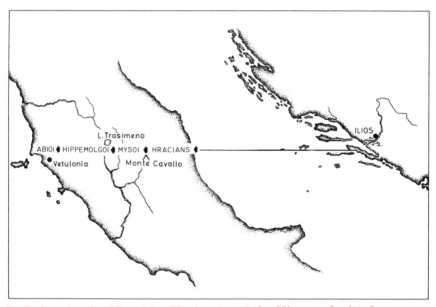

In Dalmatia, the Mysoi (or Mysians) and the Hippemolgoi (who are to
be found in the direction of a sunset) are peoples whose neighbors
are Thracians and Abioi, names which are echoed in those of Lake
Trasimeno and Vetulonia respectively.

and corroborated by the scene of a moonset, when Hera:

> . . . *darted down and left the peak of Olympos; on Pieria she stepped and lovely Emathia, and sped over the snowy mountains of the Thracian horsemen* . . .
>
> XIV, 226

But the name of the Mysoi as neighbors of the Thracians is not extant in central Italy, though its former existence is inferred indirectly through an association of *mus*, 'mouse,' as a guardian of the Muses, with the name of Pieria, the would-be abode of the Muses, who were later called the Pierides. But Pieria sounds like the interpolation of a bungling historian wishing to credit the Pieria of Thessally with literary loftiness, and so the Pieria of central Italy should read Pereia (classical Perusia, modern Perugia), where:

> . . . *of horses best by far were the mares of the son of Pheres* . . . *These had Apollo of the silver bow reared in Pereia* . . .
>
> II, 763

If the connection of the Mysoi with Pereia through an association of the root *mus* with Muses is tenuous, it is perhaps strengthened by an inverse argument of an association of the Mysoi with horses—*and* with mules:

> . . . *which on a time the Mysoi had given to Priam, a splendid gift.*
>
> XXIV, 278

Indeed!

7. TOWNS

No site is available in Asia Minor to answers for Macar, regardless of the specific geographical context mentioned in association with the island of Lesbos:

> . . . *And of thee, old sire, we hear that of old thou wast blest; how of all that toward the sea Lesbos, the seat of Macar, encloseth, and Phrygia in the up-land, and the boundless Hellespont, over all these folk, men say, thou, old sire, was preeminent* . . .
>
> XXIV, 543

The name of Macar is regarded as that of a person (so in the best manuscripts, though some consign 'a blessed, happy people'). Consequently, there is no need of identifying the name with a place in Asia Minor. But the Loeb translation (above) makes a note that Macar was a legendary king of Lesbos; likewise, the index in the Oxford text shows it to be the name of a person, and not a toponym.

However, the above quote is mistranslated, and should read thus:

> . . . as far as Lesbos above, Mácaros the seat, encloses within also Phrygia on the upper side and the boundless Hellespont . . .

Now, Lesbos is not above, nor on the upper side. It is down, and on the lower side. Mácaros is treated in the Loeb mistranslation as if it were Macáros, a noun of the 3rd declension, in the genitive case (as Liddell and Scott give in their *Lexicon*). Hence it is rendered as 'the seat of Macar' and therefore the name of a person, though the text in the Loeb and Oxford editions shows Mácaros with the accent on the

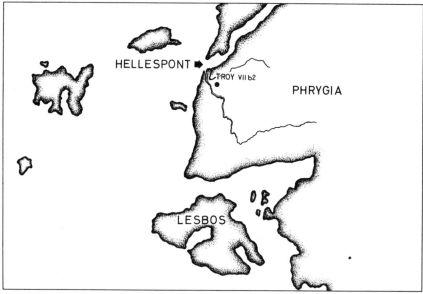

In Asia Minor, the second declension name of Mácaros, which is that of a place, and mentioned as the seat of Lesbos, is non-existent (excepting as a name recently given to an archaeological site). Furthermore, Lesbos is said to be 'above' and on the 'upper side,' and it is not: it is 'down' and on the 'lower side.'

first syllable, as a noun of the 2nd declension in the nominative case, which should then be rendered as 'Mácaros the seat (or 'abode')' in keeping as a toponym with Lesbos, Phrygia, and Hellespont, that are also in the nominative case.

The argument hinges on the position of an accent: the original Mácaros probably became the incorrect Macáros due to a scribal mistake in the copying of a text, perhaps on the strength of the treatment already given in:

"*Oh,* happy-one *son of Atreus, child of fortune . . .*"

III, 182

(which indeed is in the 3rd declension) and conveniently lent itself for a required interpretation when the Homeric Ilios was transferred to the site of TROY VIII. But, that some editor of the *Iliad,* from which we have our version, correctly placed the accent on the first syllable shows clearly that he distinguished between a 2nd and 3rd declension noun, which necessarily altered the sense of the text, and that he may very well have distinguished between an Asia Minor and Dalmatian Ilios.

Some texts have survived even with *macáron,* in the genitive plural, such as the one quoted by Plutarch in his *MORALIA, On Exile,* 603, D:

All that Lesbos bounds toward the sea, seat of the blest . . .

And Strabo, though misquoting Homer, says in his *Geography,* VIII. 3. 31:

. . . Stesichoros, they explain, uses the term "city" for the territory called Pisa, just as Homer calls Lesbos the "city of Macar" . . .

In the geographical context of a Dalmatian setting, the name of Mácaros is still extant as a toponym under the form of Makarska, a small beach resort on the mainland opposite the island of Brac where:

. . . *as far as Lesbos above, Mácaros the seat, encloses within . . .*

XXIV, 543

Fodor's Modern Guides, *YUGOSLAVIA* (David McKay Co., Inc., N.Y.: 1964) says the following about this place (pp. 181–2):

This small coastal plain [Makarska Riviera] ends abruptly at the foot of the impressive Biokovo Mountains.
. . . Makarska, since it gives its name to the district, is its "capital".

... Makarska, closed in towards the sea by mountains, might perhaps be unpleasantly hot in high summer ...

That Mácaros, as it is said, was named after a king Macar may well be so; and it is also said the island of Vis took the name after his daughter, Issa.

8. PLACES

In Homer, the difference between a *place* and a *site* is that a place is innominate and is described by a number of words, as a circumlocution, so to speak, whereas a site has a toponym, a one-word geographical statement to suit a topological peculiarity. For example: though *the ford in the Scamander,* may be a precise place, there is no one-word toponym for it, as there is for Batieïa, a site in the Scamandrian Plain from which the Danaan landings were observed by the Trojans.

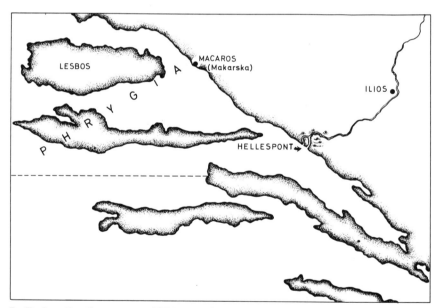

In Dalmatia, the name of Mácaros is extant in that of Makarska, a small beach resort on the mainland, 'as far as Lesbos (Brač) above,' located in 'Phrygia on the upper side.'

The point to be made is that the topology of the Asia Minor Troy is such as to considerably demean the text in detriment to the reader, since certain events are made to occur at places which, because of their ill-suited location, pass as irrelevant.

Take, for instance, the place where Hera stayed her horses:

> *But when they were come to the land of Troy and the two flowing rivers, where the Simoïs and the Scamander join their streams, there the goddess, white-armed Hera, stayed her horses, and loosed them from the car, and shed thick mist upon them; and Simoïs made ambrosia to spring up for them to graze upon.*
>
> · V, 774

Since the Simoïs does not flow into the Scamander, but rather, runs a course parallel with it prior to debouching, it is difficult to understand where, precisely, Hera stayed her horses. One naturally assumes the place must be in the marshes between the mouths of the Scamander and the Simoïs or even *in* the Hellespont, which, on a strict interpretation of the text, is:

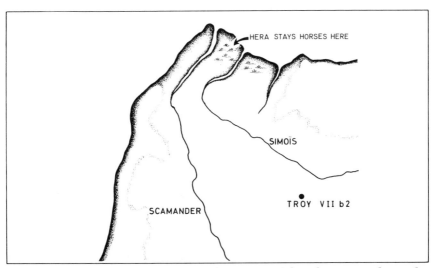

In Asia Minor, the place where Hera stayed her horses—where the Simoïs and the Scamander join their waters—must be the Hellespont, which suggests that the text's authorship was not acquainted with the terrain at all.

> . . . *where Simoïs and Scamander join their streams . . .*
>
> ibid.

But regardless of this difficulty, the reader fails to see why Simoïs (and why not Scamander?):

> . . . *made ambrosia to spring up for them to graze upon . . .*
>
> ibid.

At most, one can only venture the guess that ambrosia is common to stables, as when:

> . . . *There* [Aegae] *Poseidon, the Shaker of Earth, stayed his horses, and loosed them from the car, and cast before them food ambrosial to graze upon . . .*
>
> XIII, 35

In the geographical context of a Dalmatian setting, the place where:

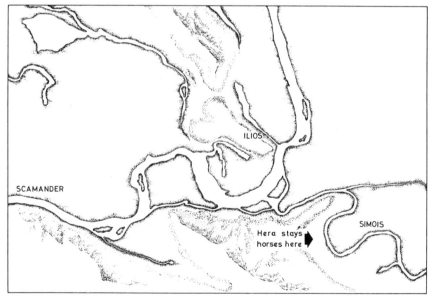

In Dalmatia, Hera stayed her horses at a natural pen formed by a V-shaped niche in the hillside shut in by the Simoïs, not unlike Priam's stables at Ilios formed by the intersection of its northern and western slopes.

> *. . . the Simoïs and the Scamander join their streams, there the*
> *goddess, white-armed Hera stayed her horses . . .*
>
> V, 774

is where the Simoïs makes an inverted S-twist to clear a rib-like promontory just before debouching opposite the southeastern spur of Ilios.
This promontory contains a natural C-shaped pen, or byre, formed by
the surrounding hillside slopes. It is evident, because of the pen's location, it was Simoïs, and not Scamander, who:

> *. . . made ambrosia to spring up for them to graze upon.*
>
> loc. cit.

The function of this place as a pen is corroborated—and enhanced—
by the anecdote of Simoïsius' birth:

> *. . . whom on a time his mother had born beside the banks of*
> *Simoïs, as she journeyed down from Ida, whither she had fol-*
> *lowed with her parents to see their flocks. For this cause they*
> *called him Simoïsius;*
>
> IV, 475

The flocks, *méla*, consisted of 'sheep' or 'goats, small cattle' and were
penned, as Hera's horses were, at the place best suited along the banks
of the Simoïs for holding animals.

The question of an association of ambrosia with stables suggests a
connection between mushrooms and manure, and so it is apropos that
Simoïs, which means 'snub-nosed', should have been a culture-medium
for ambrosia; to judge from the blue light in the grotto of Aegae, ambrosia, a word akin with the Indian *ambrita*, which is said to be a
heavenly dew that solidifies into sapphires, may be a blue mushroom.
And that it is blue, suggests again that some chemical component has
the propensity of capturing oxygen molecules, and consequently, when
ingested, of restricting oxygen flow to the brain, thus causing vividly
colored hallucinations. This would explain why ambrosia was fed to
horses (that is, mares) at Aegae, and at the pen where Siomoïsius was
born, for the females of the flock will have metabolized the harsh hallu-
cinogenic agent in the mushroom, and produced a refined agent in
their milk for a softer, and smoother high. Certainly, that Simoïsius
was born here, adds (cruelly) not only to the intended sense of an in-
creased flock of penned animals, but also to a connection of ambrosia
with lactation.

PART III

CHAPTER 5

A BRIEF DESCRIPTION OF TROY

The principle of classification of Homeric geonyms is synonymous with orderly information: classification of geonyms adjusts geographical information to what is required, and what is required is merely to understand how and why these geonyms have been used. But one perceives, from an historian's point of view that facts, as Homer would have them, have been willfully accommodated to suit a purpose. Yet this is a problem external to the recognition of what the *Iliad's* internal parameters are for the structure of a *geographical syntax*.

A description of Troy (in the broad sense of a nation), is adduced from an examination of those geonyms which carry the implicit sense of territorial extension that define political boundaries (for example, an island, but not a mountain). Thus, from the eight different classifications into which the group of geonyms 4. TROY fall, those geonyms accorded to *islands* and *districts* suit the purpose of defining the physical extension of Troy's boundaries.

Only ten territorial-extension type names are used in the text of the *Iliad* to make up a nation called Troy. These are in three sub-ordinate categories—from greater to lesser—according to the following schematic arrangement:

TROY

PHRYGIA	DARDANIA
ASCANIA	

TROY (properly Troia)

The name for the whole as a nation, which in turn is made up of three major districts which are Phrygia, Ascania and Dardania. Whatever the truth about the origin of the name of Troy, the Homeric treatment is a philological connection with its geographical *division* into *three* districts. Phrygia and Ascania fall respectively to the northern and southern districts of the seaboard, and Dardania to the mainland.

The Seaboard:

It will be noticed the conspicuous Pelješac peninsula is innominate, and reference to it in Homeric terms can only be made as the "_____ of the Cephallenians," unlike a reference to the Lesbids of Lesbos or the Sminthians of Zacynthos. The reason for this is that, as it is

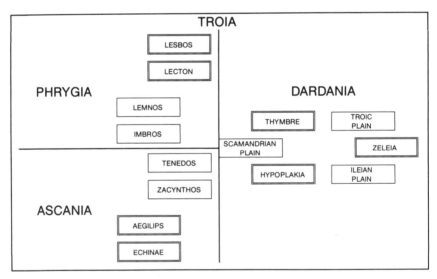

The schematic representation of district-type names for territorial extensions (not to be confused with names for islands which are a classification of their own) shows that Troia is the name for the collective whole which is divided into the three major districts of Phrygia and Ascania on the northern and southern seaboard respectively, and Dardania on the mainland. Of six sub-districts in Dardania, two sets of three names are topologically similar, of which three are near the sea, and three are inland.

not an island, it has no place in the classification of island toponymy; and as part of the mainland, its only relevance (regardless of its odd shape and the geological curiosity it is connected with the mainland by a stretch no wider than a kilometer or so) is that it is inhabited by the Cephallenians. To have named it with a a specific district-type name such as 'Cephallenia' would upset the schematic balance of the whole, and it must therefore remain innominate.

The [peninsula] of the Cephallenians stands prominent with a phallic connotation, and at once becomes the key to understanding the nomenclature for the seaboard districts, as well as that of the islands they comprise.

PHRYGIA

This district extends from the tip of the [peninsula] of the Cephallenians to the north. The name means 'brow land,' and it is so called because of its highly indented coast and many elongated islands.

Of the eight islands off the coast of Troy, four fall to Phrygia:

LESBOS, *Bratia*, Brač. The identity of Lesbos with Bratia is inferred from the island's position opposite the town of Makarska on the mainland, corresponding with the statement:

> . . . *as far as Lesbos above, Mácaros the seat, encloses within also Phrygia on the upper side and the boundless Hellespont . . .*
>
> XXIV, 543

The name is recorded before Homer in the Hittite Muwatallis letters of about 1,300 B.C. under the form of Lazpa, where some sort of magical cure was practised. That Macar, whose name means 'blessed' (as in the sense of relief from discomfort) was king of Lesbos, seems to suggests a palliative measure, as well as a connection with 'hair,' since Lesbos is cognate with *lásios*, 'shaggy with hair or wool,' 'hairy.' The original name of Macar may have been MacCar (cf. the Biblical Gog and Magog, or Og and his son MacOg), 'son of hair,' or 'born of hair,' (perhaps 'a louse'?). Little can be ventured as to what a magical cure (or even a medical one) has to do with hair, other than lice-ridden hair is shaved off. The classical name for Lesbos was Bratia (and whence the modern Brač), which some believe to have been derived from the Illyrian *brentos*, meaning 'stag;' but this opinion is on cue with the name of the Elaphites, meaning 'deer isles,' far to the south (see below) and Bratia is likelier to be a metathesis of the Greek *bátrachos*, which means 'frog,' to *brátachos* ('rogf').

The cult-significances of 'hair' and 'frog,' and their associations with each other, are obscure. Nevertheless, they appear to crop up in the person of the Lesbid poetess Sappho, whose name would seem akin with the Basque *zapoa*, meaning 'toad,' suggesting she may have been severely afflicted with goitre, and was consequently an ugly, bug-eyed and hairless woman whose lack of finger-nails led her to invent strumming the lyre with a quill.

LECTON, *Lesina/Pharos*, Hvar. An educated guess is that Lecton is the name of Hvar, and not that of a town on the mainland, from which Hera and Hypnos:

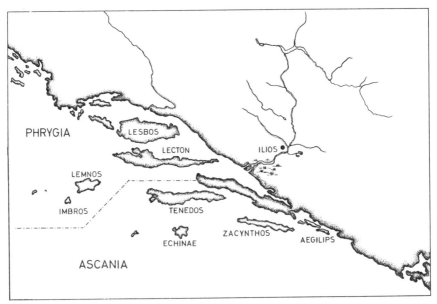

The districts of Phrygia and Ascania are separated by a long innominate peninsula on which several places of mountains and towns are known. Though it was held by the Cephallenians who derived their name from the peninsula's obvious phallic elongation, it is unwarranted to call it 'Cephallenia' (which name does not occur in the text), lest it disrupt the schematic balance of both district-type names and tribal-type names.

To many fountained Ida they came . . . even to Lecton, where first they left the sea . . .

XIV, 283

and hence. cognate with the name of *Lesina*. Pharos, whence Hvar, must be Pherae, one of the towns offered in Agamemnon's promise to Achilles:

"And seven well-peopled cities will I give him, Cardamyle, Enope, and grassy Hire and sacred Pherae and Antheia with deep meadows and fair Aepeia and vine-clad Pedasos. All are nigh to the sea on the nethermost borders of sandy Pylos."

IX, 149

Pherae is located at the western end of the island,

". . . nigh to the [open] *sea . . ."*

ibid

outside, or beyond:

". . . the nethermost borders of [the] *sandy pýlos."*

ibid

of Stonski Bay. It is probably this Pharos, and not the *light-house* at Alexandria, that Menelaos sailed to after the Trojan War.

LEMNOS, *Issa*, Viš. The reputed volcanic nature of the island is associated with Hephaistos, the smith-god, ever since the day of his birth when:

". . . the whole day long was I borne headlong, and at set of sun I fell in Lemnos, and but little life was in me. There did the Sintian folk make haste to tend me for my fall."

I, 593

The name is derived from *líme*, which is a 'humour that gathers in the corner of the eye,' 'gum,' 'rheum,' caused by furnace smoke and vapours. That Lemnos later took the name of Issa after the daughter of Macar of Lesbos, corroborates the island's association with Hephaistos, as her name is akin with the Latin *vis*, 'strength,' whence the modern name.

IMBROS, Biševo. The identity of Imbros with Biševo, which lies beside Viš, is pretty well determined by Poseidon's course from the peak of 'Samos wooded-Thracelike' to the cave of Aegae, as well as by Hera and

Hypnos' journey from the twin cities of Lemnos and Imbros to Lecton and Gargaros. Since the contiguity of Imbros with Lemnos begs for similar association of ideas as those of Lemnos, the name of Imbros may be derived from the inseparable intensive prefix *i(m)-* + *brótos* (a word of uncertain derivation and likely akin with the *ambrosia* that grew in Aegae) used in the sense of 'blood that runs from a wound' (as in the Spanish *brotar*, 'to spurt, well up'), hence 'a copious gush.' But the connection is tenuous, yet that Hera sojourned here in Hypnos' company suggests an association with death, and hence that *i(m)-* + *brótos* should read *i(m)-* + *brotós*, 'a quite mortal (man),' perhaps in reference to the delicate health of those who, like Hephaistos, were *prematurely* born.

ASCANIA

This district extends from the tip of [peninsula] of the Cephallenians to the south. The name means 'pouch country,' and it is so called because of the district's homologous association with the phallic connotations of the Pelješac peninsula.

Of the eight islands off the coast of Troy, four fall to Ascania:

TENEDOS, *Corcyra Melaina*, Korčula. The name of Tenedos is said to be eponymous of Tenes, whose story concerning certain differences of opinion with his father is a castration myth, hence *téndao* is 'to nibble at, gnaw.' But perhaps the story should be read inveresely: that Tenes took the name from Tenedos after *cutting* himself away from his father, since Tenedos is associated with the *cutting* of the island's dense forests. It was here that Agamemnon, in all likelihood, built many of the vessels listed in the *Catalogue of Ships*, and where Sinon, it is said, designed and built the fabled Trojan Horse.

Corcyra Melaina of later times derived its name in a metathesis from the town of Crocyleia listed in the *Catalogue of Ships*, whence the modern Korčula located at the eastern end of Tenedos. It was dubbed Melaina because of the island's *black* forests which gave rise to a ship-building tradition (whence the name of the *corsair*, which is not, as the O.E.D. consigns, a derivation from the Latin *currere*, 'to run').

ZACYNTHOS, *Melita*, Mljet. The name means 'very dog-like' or 'very wild dog' ('rabid'?), and probably has an association with the fact the swift mongoose roams wild over the island. To judge from the connotation of 'very wild dog,' the curse that Chryses, priest of Sminthian Apollo, inflicted upon Agamemnon's men at the onset of the *Iliad* was an epidemic of rabies, to which the mongoose is not immune. Chryses' connection with a mongoose seems likelier than Strabo's explanation that *sminthos* is an ancient word meaning 'mouse,' which would explain the particular wording of his prayer invoking a revenge:

> ". . . who dost stand over Chryse and holy Cilla, and dost rule mightily over Tenedos . . ."

I, 37

Chryses used "Tenedos" instead of the offending name "Crocyleia," lest the curse work in reverse, since Crocyleia, at the eastern end of Tenedos, would have been in schematic harmony with the names of Chryse at the eastern end of Zacynthos, and Cilla at the eastern end of Lecton. The mongoose is the natural enemy of snakes, lizards and the like, and even of *crocodiles*.

AEGILIPS, *Elaphites*, Šipan, Lopud and Koločep. The name for this short chain of three isles hugging the mainland means 'bereft even of goats,' ostensibly in reference to their utter desolation. They later became known, in keeping with their former name, as the Elaphites, which means 'deer isles.' Though the link of 'goats' with 'deer' seems like a sound identification of Aegilips with the Elaphites (whence the later Delaphodia, and the Roman name Lafota, now Lopud), the would-be Homeric meaning is unsatisfactory, for the ending *-lips* associates these isles with 'fat' and 'wind' (hence the *Li*pari or Ae*oli*ae isles are not only like blobs of fat or oil on the surface of water, but also traditionally known as islands of the wind). A*íx* means 'goat,' but the Homeric treatment of the etymology is likelier to be *aeí* 'ever' + *ge* 'earth' + *líps* 'any liquid poured forth,' 'libation,' hence 'ever land-of-libations,' indirectly suggesting that Homer has either recorded the memory of some pre-historic cult-rite performed on these islands, or that, simply, fresh water springs are to be found here.

ECHINAE, *Ladesta*, Lagosta/Lastovo. The name of this archipelago south of Tenedos means 'sea urchins,' and was perhaps so called because the innumerable boulders off its shores immediately beneath the surface of the sea elicit the same danger to wary sailors, as the urchin does to bare-footed bathers. But on the other hand, the hair-like sense of the urchin's up-right spines evokes an association with lice, as if likened to the abundant prawn peculiar to these waters, and consequently, the Latin name Ladesta evokes the Spanish *ladilla*, 'louse' as also the Italian Lagosta evokes the Spanish *langosta*, the prawn-like 'lobster'.

The Mainland:

The two distinctively contradictory features of the Dalmatian mainland are the impressive jagged heights of the barren Biokovo mountains running parallel with the length of the coast, and the flat verdant expanses of the marshy plains in the Neretva delta-valley.

DARDANIA

Dardania is the name for the mainland countryside in general, without any definite borders as a district. The six sub-districts which fall to it are restricted to the natural confines of the Scamander's valley.

SCAMANDRIAN PLAIN. This is the plain, as the name should indicate, traversed by the final portion of the Scamander's course to the sea, as well as its estuary proper. Since it is difficult to determine where, along the Scamandrian Plain, fresh water is distinguished from salt, the estuary (perhaps better called the river's *delta*) may also be referred to as the Hellespont.

Among the delta's many beautiful curiosities, one stands singularly as an out-cropping in the midst of brackish marshes, toward the delta's northern apex, which might be said to be one of the first of the Trojan topological features to be mentioned in the *Iliad*:

> *Now there is before the city a steep mound afar out in the plain, with clear space about it on this side and on that; this do men verily call Batieia, but the immortals call it the barrow of Myrine, light of step.*

II, 811

THYMBRE. The word means 'savoury,' a bitter herb used for condimenting that makes the mouth go awry. The location of this district in the area of numerous fresh water pools in the hillside indentations of the Scamandrian Plain's left bank begs for a reconsideration of the geographical meaning of the name, for if savoury grows here, there is no reason why it cannot grow elsewhere. Hence the meaning must be sought in *túmbos*, 'tomb' (that is, a *cavity* as opposed to a cairn), + *bráche*, 'shallow stagnant pool,' or in *túmbos* + *phréar*, 'a well, water tank' (Latin *puteus*). But whatever the etymology, it is certain the poor Dolon deserved the death associated with Thymbre for the witless answer he gave Odysseus:

> *"Verily now this likewise will I frankly tell thee. Towards the sea lie the Carians and the Paeonians . . . And towards Thymbre fell the lot of the Lycians and the lordly Mysians . . ."*
>
> X, 427

The statement implies that Lycian and Mysian allies of the Trojans were encamped in the very midst of the Danaans who already held Thymbre. Yet the poignant irony is in the bravado of the *double entendre* of Dolon's answer (and this must certainly raise him in one's estimation!), for Odysseus himself was the traitor, a Cephallenian Trojan among Danaans.

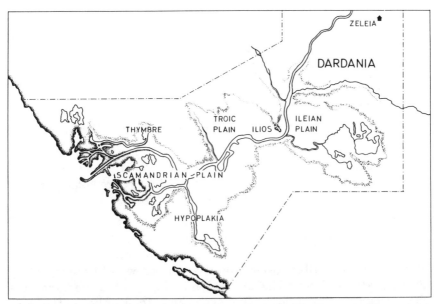

Thymbre and Hypoplakia are topologically identical and etymologically akin in the same way the Troic and Ileian Plains are. The swampy Scamandrian Plain also goes by the name Hellespont, a reduplicative-type name to accentuate its topological characteristic, derived from *helós* 'a marsh-meadow' + *póntos*, 'the sea.'

HYPOPLAKIA. 'under *plax*' ('anything flat, and broad, flat land,' also 'a flat stone, tombstone') means 'cemetery,' and is not only cognate in meaning with Thymbre but also the identical topological counterpart on the opposite side of the Scamander, exactly as the Troic and Ileian Plains are to each other in meaning and topology.

TROIC PLAIN. Almost all of the Troic Plain is marshy, with the exception of alluvial deposits which form a sort of quay on the Scamander's right bank, shutting in the marshes behind them. Consequently, overland traffic to and from Ilios and the Hellespont must take a route skirting the Troic Plain along the hillside's higher ground, as when Hector was chased by Agamemnon:

> But Hector did Zeus draw forth from the missiles and the dust
> . . . but the son of Atreus followed after . . . And past the Tomb
> of ancient Ilos, son of Dardanus, over the midst of the plain, past
> the wild fig-tree they sped, striving to win the city . . . But when
> they were come to the Scaian Gates and the oak-tree, there then
> the two hosts halted . . .

XI, 163

The Tomb of Ilos is the striking feature of a perfectly cone-shaped hill topped with ruins (perhaps of Roman origins?), immediately on the left as one enters the marshes of the Troic Plain from the Scamandrian Plain.

ILEIAN PLAIN. The wall of Heracles is mentioned in the lines:

> . . . the dark-haired god led the way to the heaped-up wall of
> godlike Heracles, the high wall that the Trojans and Pallas
> Athene had builded for him . . . and they of the other part sat
> over against them on the brows of Callicolone . . .

XX, 144

This is the Ostrovo limestone spit which separates the Ileian Plain in two, and hence the meaning of the name, 'long stone.' That Trojans, with the aid of Pallas Athene, built a natural wall-like spit, rather than a wall, need not strike one as conflicting. On the one hand, it is the geological counterpart to the cone-shaped Tomb of Ilos in the Troic Plain (ostensibly also built by Trojans); and on the other, its connection with Athene's general watery associations (as in this instance surrounded by marsh-lakes) links the spit with the Walls of Ilios which enclose the Temple of Athene on Callicolone, on the southeastern brow of Ilios.

ZELEIA. The name is an excellent one, for it evokes the *zeal* with which those who lived here emulated or resembled the Ilians, presumably because of this district's similarity with the marshy environs of Ilios. Yet this cannot really be the justification for the name, else it would be natural to suspect more attention would have been given to the name than it has. Since the common denominator of the Scamandrian, Troic and Ileian Plains is that of marshy plains, Zeleia must relate with Thymbre and Hypoplakia in the same measure, and consequently puns with *sélinon*, 'parsley' which, however, is not a geographical justification for the name (as 'savoury' is not for that of Thymbre). Zeleia therefore suggests another pun on *selís*, a 'plank,' the flat 'leaf of papyrus,' in keeping with the flatness of Thymbre and Hypoplakia as cemeteries. But again, the pun is not a correct geographical statement, and therefore the remaining alternatives for an explanation are that, on the one hand, the original Homeric was Seleia which an impudent editor of the *Iliad* changed to Zeleia for the reader's benefit of relating Seleia directly with a Trojan sub-district; or on the other, that Zeleia is to be read *Zaleia* (as in the case of Zanthos for Xanthos), meaning '(very) great plunder,' which is hoarded and buried or hoarded in caves.

Since the delta-valley of the Neretva is the only fertile district of any great consideration along the entire harsh and mountainous Dalmatian country, it has attracted peoples from the adjacent islands and immediate coastal vicinities since remotest times. This is attested by the many prehistoric sites in these regions, and the length of the Neretva's gorge, as far up as Zeleia (for here the river turns in an up-side-down-U to the east), served as a natural highway for traffic to and from the coastal regions into the interior central countries of the Balkan peninsula. It is then to be assumed the original Homeric Zaleia was so called from the local inhabitants who way-laid those passing through here with a compulsory tariff.

It would be fair to mention that a Homeric bias of the Trojan plight is an incorrect observation, for not only does the narration mention Trojan foibles and follies liberally, but also insinuates moral turpitude—as above—which shows the *Iliad* is objective and impartial (as history should be?). Furthermore, an elementary sense of strategy needfully impugns Trojan moral rectitude, for the sorry lot of those

traveling the Scamander's route to and from the coast and the hinterland were caught at one end or the other, thus accounting for
Priam's great wealth which, upon a time, may have rivaled even that of
Minyas' treasury. Obviously, there was more at stake in the formidable
Trojan War than the mere return of Helen, for the obliteration of the
stronghold of Ilios—and at that, pretty well chosen, to judge from the
length of the war—implied a definite change in the world's then balance of powers.

SCAMANDER'S RIGHT BANK WHERE DANAAN SHIPS BEACHED.

VIEW ACROSS TROIC PLAIN TOWARDS ILIOS.

THE TOMB OF ILOS.

VIEW OF WESTERN SPUR OF PERGAMOS FROM PLAIN.

CHAPTER 6

A PRELIMINARY SURVEY OF ILIOS

There remains the task of a positive identification of Gabela with the site of Homeric Ilios. I suppose one might say that Gabela is the site that best suits the Homeric account (and this is true). Also that no other site in the Neretva delta-valley is available (and this also is true). But the only way of linking Gabela with the Homeric Ilios is by showing that Homer—that is, the *Iliad's* authorship—was *intimately* acquainted with the site, and that all the details of the Homeric descriptions of Ilios can be accounted for by the particular morphology of the hillock and the extant ruins found on it.

There is nothing exceptionally spectacular about Ilios; its beauty is an esoteric one, if only because of the *Iliad's* devotion to it. It was a cult-shrine of an Iron Age people, rather than an integrated defensive site, or a 'city,' in the sense one understands *polis*. Its various parts and places had mystical associations; its shape and the cult-function of its ruins betray it as such.

The hillock of Ilios looks like a *trinacría*, but better yet, its phallic resemblance is precisely the key to the nomenclature of its *three* parts; thus one finds:

PERGAMOS

The western, and adjacent northern spur, are homologous with the testicles, and hence called Pergamos, which means 'scrotum.' The name is derived from *péra*, 'a leathern pouch,' 'wallet,' and *gémos*, 'a load,' and by extension, 'to be full of.' The Spanish word *pergamino*, meaning

'parchment,' is derived from the name of Pergamum, but not because
this place was known for the product, but because of the similar characteristics of shrinking and stretching that both parchment and the
scrotum share.

That Pergamos was the highest part of Ilios is confirmed from the
following instances, when:

> *Nor did Paris tarry long in his lofty house, but did on his
> glorious armour, dight with bronze, and hastened through the
> city . . . even so Paris, son of Priam, strode down from high
> Pergamos, all gleaming in his armour like the shining sun . . .*
>
> VI, 512

and:

> *. . . but in truth Cassandra, peer of golden Aphrodite, having
> gone up upon Pergamos, marked her dear father as he stood in
> the car . . .*
>
> XXIV, 700

[SCAIA]

The length of the southeastern spur is, in the strictest sense, innominate (as in the case of the '_____ of the Cephallenians') and does not
occur in the text. But a name for this part as [Scaia], in the nominative
singular, may be adduced grammatically from that of the Scaian Gates,
an adjectival noun in the nominative plural, which are located at the
bottom of the spur's sloping end, where access onto the hillock is gained
from the plain. The meaning of the root *scai-* is a complex matter, for it
requires positing an etymology in a language of Near Eastern origins
to account for the Homeric association of [Scaia] with the penile shaft,
and Scaian Gates with the prepuce. To seek a meaning in the association of ideas of *skaiós* (Latin *scaevus*), 'left,' 'on the left hand or side,'
with a gate on the *left* side of an *auspex* who faced north for his bird-
divining, is an understandable, though absurd proposition.

CALLICOLONE

The tip of the southeastern spur is a sudden rise above the Scaian
Gates homologous with the *glans*, hence its allusive name, 'Beauty
Hill.'

Though the shape of Ilios is like that of a three-legged sun-faced *tri-nacria*, its phallic shape invites speculation of a close association with Troy's phallic seaboard, suggesting that the *Iliad*, known to us as a heroic epic, was in fact originally conceived as a sacred text celebrating Ilios.

Callicolone is mentioned twice in the text, once when:

> *. . . over against her shouted Ares, dread as a dark whirlwind, calling with shrill tones to the Trojans from the topmost citadel, and now again as he sped to the shores of Simoeïs over Callicolone.*

XX, 53

(which shows that Callicolone is on the distal end of 'the topmost citadel' of Pergamos, and opposite the place across the Scamander where Simoeïs debouches), and once again, when:

> *. . . the dark-haired god led the way to the heaped-up wall of godlike Heracles, the high wall that the Trojans and Pallas Athene had builded for him . . . and they of the other part sat over against them on the brows of Callicolone . . .*

XX, 144

which corroborates the identity of Callicolone with the tip of the southeastern spur, in this incidental reference to Laomedon's wall along the perimeter of the hill, on which one may stand and browse on the surrounding countryside.

The table below shows the locations and relative positions of the various buildings described in the text which are answered not only by the morphology proper to the hillock, but by their extant remains as well:

PERGAMOS

1. PALACE OF PRIAM (SANCTUARY OF APOLLO)	Oval platform of a megalithic observatory on the summit of the western spur.
2. PROTHYRON AND ECHOING PORTICO	Landing at intersection of adjacent spurs, and lanes along the sides of concave slopes.
3. PRIAM'S STABLES	The plain enclosed by slopes of intersecting spurs.
4. ROOMS OF ALEXANDER	L-shaped construction in several terraced levels on the summit of the northern spur.

[SCAIA]

5. CITY AND CENTRAL AVENUE — Modern town traversed by central road with several side-streets.

6. HOUSES OF HECTOR AND HECABE — Mound (uninvestigated) on dividing line between Pergamos and [Scaia].

7. THALAMOS TREASURE CHAMBER AND SWINGING DOORS — Site inferred from partial tracings at the bottom of southeastern spur.

8. SCAIAN GATES — Main access onto the hillock from the plain on either side of spur.

CALLICOLONE

9. WALLS OF ILIOS — Massive walls along the perimeter of southeastern promontory.

10. SANIDE GATE — Access in walls leading up from Scaian Gates to the enclosure on summit of the southeastern promontory.

11. PLACE OF WATCH — Remains of a construction on western corner of walls overlooking the Scaian Gates.

12. TEMPLE OF ATHENE — Enclosure within walls and inferred site of sacred well (a tannery?).

13. THEANO'S GATE — Cloacal exit (sluice gate?) on the face of southeastern wall.

1. PALACE OF PRIAM (SANCTUARY OF APOLLO)

On the summit of the western spur is the (apparently) intact oval platform of what was once a megalithic observatory. Its major axis aligns in the direction of the midwinter sunrise, with an azimuth of 123°19′. In the center of the platform, facing the midwinter sunrise, is the small, modern church of Sveti Stephan. A short distance behind it are the remains of a rectangular construction, perhaps upon a time a Roman sentry's look-out post (and, it seems, later enlarged and used during the Turkish domination). A number of rather large, solidly embedded

rocks in the surrounding rubble might possibly be the markers once
used for reckoning positions along the horizon (and, I dare say, in their
original position?). But an exact survey of the site and archaeological
repairs are wanting before any commitment can be made on this wise.

This site corresponds to the place where:

> *Aeneas then did Apollo set apart from the throng in sacred*
> *Pergamos where was his temple* [neós] *builded. There Leto and*
> *the archer Artemis healed him in the great sanctuary* [megalón
> ádyton], *and glorified him . . .*

> V, 446

The observatory is described with detail when Hector:

> *. . . was now come to the beauteous palace* [dómos] *of Priam,*
> *adorned with polished sun halls* [áithousai] *and in it were fifty*
> *chambers* [thálamoi] *of polished stone, built each hard by the*
> *other; therein the sons of Priam were wont to sleep beside their*
> *wedded wives; and for his daughters over against them on the*
> *opposite side within the court* [aulé] *were twelve roofed cham-*
> *bers* [tégeoi thálamoi] *of polished stone, built each hard by the*
> *other; therein slept Priam's sons-in-law beside their chaste*
> *wives . . .*

> VI, 242

The *áithousai* 'sun halls,' so called because they catch the *warm* sun-
light, must be a megalithic observatory's two circular sets of up-right
markers required for the sighting of positions along the horizon (not
unlike the sights of a gun barrel) and so 'catch' the sun's seasonal positions at the moment of sunrise or sunset.

That there were:

> *. . . fifty chambers* [thálamoi] *of polished stone, built each hard*
> *by the other . . .*

> ibid.

corresponds with an outer ring or set of markers, perhaps arranged in
a circle at equidistant intervals from each other or at certain precise
and necessary points. The number fifty is one traditionally associated
with progeny, but it is also the number of lunations in a four year
period ($50 \times 29.5 = 1,475$ days; $4 \times 365 = 1,460$ days), and so the outer
ring of markers would seem to be associated with the moon, not unlike
the function of the 56 holes in the Aubrey Circle at Stonehenge.

And that:

> . . . *over against them on the opposite side within the court*
> [aulé] *were twelve roofed chambers* [tégeoi thálamoi] *of pol-*
> *ished stone* . . .
>
> ibid.

corresponds with an inner ring or set of markers, perhaps arranged in
the shape of a horseshoe, and aligned with the platform's major axis
in the direction of the midwinter sunrise. Now, the sons' fifty *thálamoi*
do not necessarily preclude a roof, yet, the daughters' twelve *tégeoi*
thálamoi is an obvious allusion to the twelve zodiacal constellations
representing a 'house' on the ecliptic.

The position of certain prominent stones standing out among the
rubble looks queer. Their distinction from the general homogenous ap-
pearance of the debris makes them suspect, and invites one to specu-
late they may be a number of remaining 'chambers of polished stone,'

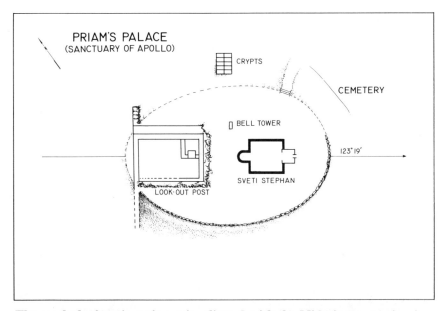

**The oval platform's major axis, aligned with the Midwinter sunrise, is a
give-away for the identification of Priam's Palace (the Sanctury of Apollo) as a megalithic observatory. This explains the fifty of his sons'
chambers around twelve of his daughters' 'roofed' chambers as concentric sets of outer and inner stone markers set up for seasonal obser-
vations. On the platform were later superimposed a Roman (Turkish?)
look-out post and, recently, the little church of Sveti Stephan.**

having survived demolition because of their incorporation within the
look-out post's building plans. Others which had no architectural function related to the building were cleared away to make room for whatever, and are no longer extant.

The identical archaeological counterpart to this megalithic observatory is Sarmizegetusa, near the village of Grădiste, in Rumania,
which consists of a round platform, an outer ring, and an inner horseshoe aligned with the midwinter sunrise. Yet the Homeric description
of the Palace of Priam, which was the Sanctuary of Apollo, calls for a
lesser number of markers, suggesting it may have been a neater instrument, reduced to its simplest elements: 'elegant,' as in the sense of
a neat solution to a mathematical problem.

2. PROTHYRON AND ECHOING PORTICO

The landing at the intersection of the western and northern spurs,
where a short lane and a long trail leading up from Priam's Stables
converge, also opens the way to the Palace of Priam on the summit of
the western spur, the Rooms of Alexander on the summit of the northern spur, and to the City and Central Avenue along the lower length of
the southeastern spur. Its function (which might be said to be the axis
about which the *trinacría* shape of Ilios spins) is that of a *vestibulum*,
and hence the name *próthyron*, which means 'place before the gates:'

> Then the old man made haste and stepped upon his car, and
> drave forth from the gateway [próthyron] and the echoing por-
> tico [aithoúsa eridoúpou] . . . But when they had gone down
> from the city and were come to the plain, back then to Ilios
> turned his sons and daughters' husbands . . .
>
> XXIV, 322

The 'echoing portico,' *aithoúsa eridoúpou*, is explained by the convex
or amphitheatre-like slopes of the intersecting spurs, which form a
kind of 'hall' and capture all sounds from Priam's Stables below, perhaps even magnifying them.

3. PRIAM'S STABLES

The plain between the adjacent western and northern spurs of Pergamos is a natural V-shaped pen. It is neatly outlined by a low stone

wall whose foundations rest on the hillside's slopes about a meter below ground level. There lead up two lanes from this pen, along either side of the spurs, and converge on the Prothyron at the top. The shorter lane, along the side of the western spur, has been well-trodden, and sections at various intervals on the way up have been lined on the hillside with a low-lying containing wall. The other lane, along the side of the northern spur, is a longer trail, and at a lesser slant (as observed from a distance), and wide enough to accommodate an automobile.

This pen is naturally suited for containing animals, and must be the place where Priam kept his horses:

> "Will ye not make me ready a waggon, and that with·speed, and lay all these things therein, that we may get forward on our way?"
>
> So spake he, and they, seized with fear . . . brought forth the light-running waggon drawn of mules . . . And for Priam they

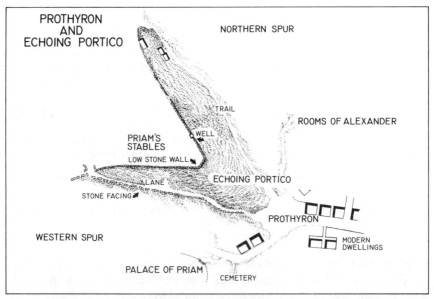

The angular niche formed by the intersection of the adjacent spurs of Pergamos is naturally suited for stabling horses. A lane and trail lead up from the plain on either side of the spurs to the Prothyron, a gateway which opens onto several parts on Ilios. The Echoing Portico (or Noisy Sun Hall) is the amphitheatre-like intersection of the slopes.

*led beneath the yoke horses that the old king kept for his own
and reared at the polished stall.*

XXIV, 263

The mule-drawn wagon and horses fetched by Priam's sons were
likely brought up to him through the longer trail, for the shorter one is
certainly too narrow. That the stall was 'polished' means simply that
the pen's V-shape was a neatly contoured stone wall.

4. ROOMS OF ALEXANDER

On the summit of the northern spur is a quadrangular set of terraced
ruins resembling two rectangles laid on each other at right ᴗngles, like
a letter **L**; the building has been leveled off into plots with refills contained by high walls of closely knit hewn stone.

These ruins answer to the description of the Rooms of Alexander,
to wit:

> *. . . but Hector went his way to the rooms of Alexander* [pròs
> dómat Alexándroio]; *the fair ones that himself had builded
> with men that were in that day the best builders in deep-soiled
> Troy; these had made him a chamber* [thálamon] *and a room*
> [dóma] *and court* [aulén] *hard by Priam and Hector in the city
> height* [en pólei ákre].

VI, 313

Now, the rooms are described as having a chamber, a room, and a
court, but this does not agree with a statement elsewhere, when:

> *She found Helen in the hall* [megáron] *where she was weaving a
> great purple web of double fold, and thereon was broidering
> many battles of the horse-taming Trojans and brazen-coated
> Achaeans . . .*

III, 125

which implies, by the use of the added word *megáron*, there was still a
fourth unit, a hall, to be incorporated with the Rooms of Alexander, yet
inconsistent with the subsequent references to them:

> *. . . and straightway she veiled herself with shining linen, and
> went forth from her chamber* [thalámoio] . . .

III, 141

> *But him Aphrodite snatched up . . . and set him down in his*
> *fragrant, vaulted chamber* [thalámo euódei keóenti] . . .
>
> III, 380

> *"Come hither; Alexander calleth thee to go to thy home. There is*
> *he in his chamber* [thalámo] *and on his inlaid couch, gleaming*
> *with beauty . . ."*
>
> III, 390

> *Now when they were come to the beautiful room of Alexan-*
> *der . . . she, the fair lady, went to the high-roofed chamber*
> [hypsórophon thalámon].
>
> III, 421

The explanation, as I see it, for using still a fourth name for one of
the three units in the Rooms of Alexander is that, while the sense of
dómata, in the plural, carries a collective connotation of a 'building'

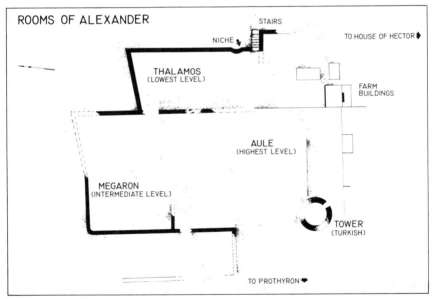

**The Rooms of Alexander are now three earth-filled terraced levels. The
identity of the *aulé* as that of a foyer seems obvious, and that of the
mégaron, from which Helen went to and fro, is confirmed by a set of
steps. The walls, built of evenly sized hewn stone, appear to be by the
same hand that erected the walls on Callicolone.**

(and indeed, the word is derived from *démo*, 'to build, construct'), the
singular form, *dóma*, can only mean a part of that building, that is, a
space of it, or a 'room,' and is therefore nothing more than an undetermined unit; the three rooms, then, are a *mégaron*, a *thalámos*, and
an *aulé*.

The question remains, which of the three names for the units corresponds with each of the three terraced plots? This is a riddle to be
solved in the following manner:

First, is the problem of establishing in what sequence the plots are to
be named: from the top left, down, and to the right, or in the inverse
order (but not, say, from the lower right up to the top left, and then
down).

Second, is the problem of establishing in which order the rooms are
to be named; thus, to the original sequence of a *thálamos*, a *dóma*, and
an *aulé*, is added the fourth, a *mégaron*, and the superfluous *dóma*
deleted.

The two possible identities of the plots are:

ROOM	A	B
Upper left: Center: Lower right:	*thálamos* *aulé* *mégaron*	*mégaron* *aulé* *thálamos*

The correct order should be choice B, on the strength of a stairway
incorporated with the walls which lead one off around the back way,
along the eastern slope of Pergamos, onto the Central Avenue. This
would account for Helen's departure from, and return to, the Rooms of
Alexander via the *thálamos*, and not the *aulé* which leads directly onto
the Prothyron.

Perhaps it is redundant to mention that the identity of the ruins on
the northern spur with the Rooms of Alexander is corroborated in two
instances; once, by their location:

> . . . *hard by* [the places of] *Priam and Hector in the city height*
> [en pólei ákre].

VI, 316

and again, by the scene of the foolish Paris, when:

> *Nor did Paris tarry long in his lofty house, but did on his*
> *glorious armour, dight with bronze, and hastened through the*
> *city . . . even so, Paris, son of Priam, strode down from high*
> *Pergamos . . .*

VI, 503

5. CITY AND CENTRAL AVENUE

The modern lay-out and haphazard distribution of buildings and
streets on the southeastern spur of Gabela cannot be too different from
the former distribution of dwellings on [Scaia] along either side of a
Central Avenue and its side-streets. The dwellings will have been of an
undetermined number and of an unspecified sort, evidently allotted to
members of Priam's family for cult reasons.(see below). Most likely, the
common-folk were excluded from the right to a habitation and rele-
gated to living quarters elsewhere, since, the enormous number of
Trojans seeking refuge from the Danaans' onslaught may well have
been accommodated within the walls, but certainly not in dwellings on
a permanent basis.

6. HOUSES OF HECTOR AND HECABE

There are two notable exceptions to the homogenous quality and value
of the dwellings on [Scaia]: one is the House of Hector, and the other of
Hecabe, which, because of the preeminence of their dwellers, are symbolic of other, similar dwellings
     There is enough information in the text on both these houses (consid-
erably more than of others which are simply mentioned in passing) to
identify the site of Hector's House with a mound in the second quadrant of the coordinates formed by the border of Pergamos with [Scaia]
and the Central Avenue. Likewise, in keeping with a desirable sense of
symmetry, the House of Hecabe is somewhere on the steep slopes of the
third quadrant.
     The House of Hector cannot be elsewhere than in the second quad-
rant, since the Rooms of Alexander were:

> *. . . hard by* [the places of] *Priam and Hector in the city height*
> [en pólei ákre].

VI, 316

showing all three places to have been equidistant. Furthermore, since
there is no place on Pergamos for the House of Hector, the site for it
must then necessarily fall towards the upper part of [Scaia], on the
border with Pergamos. This is confirmed when Hector, leaving his own
house, passes through the City before coming to the Scaian Gates:

> . . . *Hector of the flashing helm departed* [from the Rooms of
> Alexander] *and came speedily to his well-built house* [dómous].
> *But he found not white-armed Andromache in his halls*
> [megároi] . . . *So Hector, when he found not his peerless wife
> within, went and stood upon the threshold* [oudós], *and spake
> amid the serving women* . . .
>
> . . . *and Hector hastened from the house back onto the same*

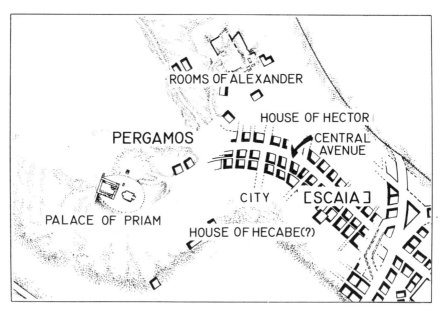

**The House of Hector, equidistant from the Palace of Priam and the
Rooms of Alexander, will have to be found on the border line between
Pergamos and [Scaia], where the Central Avenue turns to the left. The
steep slopes are ill-suited for a House of Hecabe, which invites speculation that it must be sought as a well or spring at the base of Ilios.**

*way along the well-built streets. When now he was come to the
gates, as he passed through the great city, the Scaian, whereby
he was minded to go forth to the plain . . .*

VI, 369

Here a key word is *oudós*, 'the threshold or entrance to any place,'
which is a borderline distinguishing the outside from the inside, and
by the same token, the one side from the other. That the entrance to the
House of Hector (the threshold) should have been on the Central
Avenue suits the sense well that Hector:

. . . departed [from the Rooms of Alexander] *and came speedily
to his well-built house . . .*

ibid.

but not finding Andromache within:

*. . . hastened from the house back on to the same way along the
well-built streets.*

ibid.

But the use of the plural 'streets' for the Central Avenue suggests
Hector used a back way that leads from the Rooms of Alexander onto
the Central Avenue—the one Helen used when she issued from her
thálamos on her way to The Place of Watch on the wall—which in fact
exists, precisely on the borderline of [Scaia] and Pergamos. This lends
the idea of an *oudós* as an entrance from a side street, rather than that
of a gate or doorway on the Central Avenue.

Now, whereas the site for the House of Hector in the second quadrant
is signaled by a mound, peculiar to the topological contours of the
hillock which deflects the course of the Central Avenue slightly to the
left before coming onto the Prothyron, no such vestige of the House of
Hecabe is to be found in the third quadrant, ill-suited for a building of
any preponderance because of the hillside's steep inclination.

Here then is the Homeric solution for the mention of both houses: all
dwellings on [Scaia] are the same—indistinct and indistinguishable—
but the House of Hecabe, which for the sake of symmetry must be of
equal importance to the House of Hector, must then be located in the
immediate vicinity of a most unlikely place where the hillside is
almost sheer. The conjecture to be drawn to account for the lack of any
remains of the House of Hecabe, is that both these houses are to be
thought of as complementary positive (male) and negative (female)

topological values, as if one existed and the other did not. But it is not like Homer to give an account of something that is not, and therefore some other explanation must be sought.

Perhaps vestiges of a well (representing a negative topological value) should be sought at the base of the hillock, from which lustral waters could be drawn up to the Palace of Priam. Such a well, precisely at the niche where the western spur of Pergamos and [Scaia] meet (a place not unlike that of Priam's Stables) would account for Hecabe's offer to Hector:

> But when he was now come to the beauteous Palace of Priam . . .
> there his bounteous mother came to meet him . . . "But stay till I
> have brought thee honey-sweet wine . . .
>   "Bring me no honey-hearted wine, honoured [pótnia] mother
> . . . moreover with hands unwashen I have awe to pour libation
> of flaming wine to Zeus . . .
>
> VI, 242

That Hecabe is referred to as *pótnia* gives her a watery association. Furthermore, the sense of Hecabe mistakenly drawing honey-hearted wine rather than lustral waters is insinuated in Hector's polite rebuff that she would do as well by going to the Temple of Athene.

7. THALAMOS TREASURE-CHAMBER
AND SWINGING DOORS

One must posit the former existence of a subterranean passage in the vicinity of the Scaian Gates, which is inferred from the instance when:

> But the queen herself went down [from her hall and the city] to·
> the vaulted treasure-chamber [thálamon katabéseto keóenta]
> wherein were her robes, richly broidered . . . Of these Hecabe
> took one . . . Then she went her way.
>
> VI, 288

And again, when:

> And himself he went down [from the Palace of Priam] to the
> vaulted treasure-chamber [thálamon katabéseto keóenta], fra-
> grant of cedar wood and high of roof [kédrinon hypsórophon]
> that held jewels many . . .
>
> XXIV, 191

But no such chamber exists now in the vicinity of the Scaian Gates. Yet, what might be construed as traces of its former existence is betrayed by the angular course of a side street, peculiar to the topology of this area, suggesting that a subterranean passage would have run the course of the street in a trapeze under the Central Avenue, with an entrance at either end.

It would seem a trapeze is the required shape of a tunnel-like treasure chamber, and this is confirmed when:

> *Then drave he all the Trojans from out the portico* [aithoúsa],
> *and chid them with words of reviling . . .*

XXIV, 237

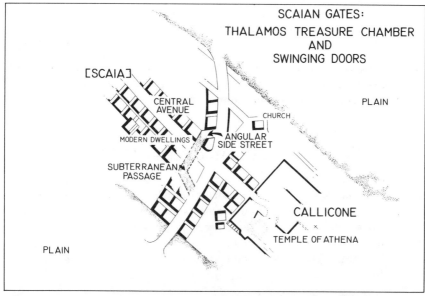

The need of positing the former existence of a Thalamos Treasure Chamber with a pair of automatically Swinging Doors as a subterranean passage in the vicinity of the Scaian Gates, is derived from the inference of their location on the lower slopes of Ilios. Its trapezoidal shape, in keeping with the banking sense of *trápeza*, is adduced from the angle of a side street as one of its two former entrances. The Scaian Gates may be thought of, like the Prothyron at the top, as a complex of gates giving access to different parts.

as the use of the word *aithoúsa* (as in the case of the Echoing Portico
and the halls in the Palace of Priam), suggests an irregular or oval-
esque shape. Also, a trapeze goes with the banking sense of a treasure-
chamber: *trapeza* is a 'table,' because of its shape, and also 'bank,' because, like the slanted legs of a table, the trapeze-shaped doors of a
bank are hinged aslant so they may never remain open, and automatically swing shut (hence, by extension, the Spanish *banco*, is both a
'bench' and a 'bank').

That the Thalamos Treasure Chamber might, in fact, have been fitted with such a set of automatically shutting doors, is adduced from the
instance when:

> *Forthwith he [Zeus] sent an eagle, surest of omen among winged
> birds, the dusky eagle, even the hunter, that men call also the
> black eagle. Wide as is the door of some rich man's high-roofed
> treasure-chamber, a door well fitted with bolts, even so wide
> spread his wings to this side and to that.*

XXIV, 315

The eagle is the constellation Aquila, whose stars Alshain and Tarazed
flank Altair, as would the two hypothetical entrances to the Treasure
Chamber on either side of the Central Avenue.

8. SCAIAN GATES

Access onto Ilios from the plain was gained, as it still is today, through
the Scaian Gates located at the bottom of [Scai], whence their name.
But one may think of the Scaian Gates as an *area*, rather than as gates
per se. This area runs like a wide street, from one side of the plain to
the other over the width of [Scaia], more or less perpendicular to the
Central Avenue. The gates themselves are a *complex* of three sorts of
pairs, thus:

- Northern and southern accesses from the plain.
- Left and right doors to the Treasure Chamber.
- Entrances to [Scaia] and to Callicolone.

The name for this area is confirmed in the instances when:

> . . . *now he was come to the gates, as he passed through the great
> city, the Scaian, whereby he was minded to go forth to the
> plain* . . .

VI, 392

And when:

> ... *even so Paris ... strode down from high Pergamos ...*
> *Speedily then he overtook goodly Hector ...*
>
> VI, 512

> ... *glorious Hector hastened forth from the gates, and with him*
> *went his brother Alexander ...*
>
> VII, 1

The gates to and from the plain seem to have been distinguished from each other by their respective association with an oak and a fig tree. Three instances in the text confirm an oak at the Scaian Gates (ostensibly the southern access from the plain):

> *But when Hector was come to the Scaian Gates and the oak tree,*
> *round about him came running the wives and daughters of the*
> *Trojans ...*
>
> VI, 237

> "... *Hector had no mind to rouse battle far from the wall, but*
> *would come only so far as the Scaian Gates and the oak tree ..."*
>
> IX, 354

> *But when they were come to the Scaian Gates and the oak tree,*
> *there then the two hosts halted and awaited each other.*
>
> XI, 170

But there is an alternate reading for 'oak tree' as *pýrgos*, '(construction on a) wall,' (hence 'a tower'), and the question of which of the two words is the better, more desirable, becomes a tricky matter. Whichever the choice, it is apt, and obviously betrays an editor's knowledge of the site of Ilios. If 'oak tree' is the interpolation, it is to distinguish this gate from the other associated with a fig tree. But if 'tower' is the interpolation, it is lent by Priam's look-out post on the walls over the Scaian Gates:

> *And they that were about Priam ... sat as elders of the people*
> *over the Scaian Gates ... like unto cicalas that in a forest sit*
> *upon a tree and pour forth their lily-like voices, even in such*
> *wise sat the leaders of the Trojans upon the wall.*
>
> III, 149

Perhaps a fig tree is made to distinguish the northern access onto the plain from the one associated with an oak or a tower, simply because it happens that fig trees are peculiar to the area behind a small church

beneath the walls, and grow in abundance—indeed, as nowhere else on
Gabela—as naturally as moss grows on the north side of trees:

> *Past the place of watch, and the wind-waved wild fig-tree they*
> *sped, ever away from under the wall along the waggon-track,*
> *and came to the two fair-flowing fountains, where well up the*
> *two springs that feed eddying Scamander.*

XXII, 145

9. WALLS OF ILIOS

The summit of Callicolone is enclosed by an almost rectangular set of
walls running along the hill's perimeter. They are of varying heights at
different points, owing to the uneven level of their foundations, though

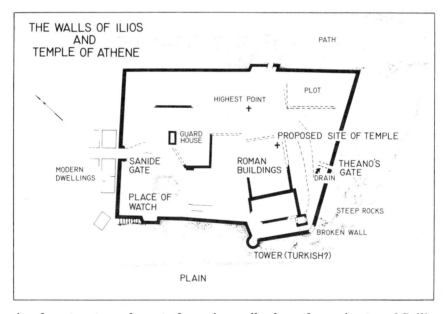

An almost rectangular set of massive walls along the perimeter of Callicolone enclose the Temple of Athene, and is broken at the Scaian Gates
by the Sanide Gate, and at the distal end, by the cloacal exit of Theano's
Gate. The construction of a fortress-like building (of Roman origins?)
was later incorporated in part of the southwestern length of the wall,
which has been partially refaced and a round tower (from the Turkish
domination?) add to it.

their top appears to be generally level, and the enclosure flat, with the exception of a corner which has crumbled and allowed the soil to erode.

The story of their construction is a puzzle:

> . . . what time we came at the bidding of Zeus and served the Lordly Laomedon for a year's space at a fixed wage, and he was our taskmaster and laid on us his commands. I verily built for the Trojans round about their city a wall, wide and exceedingly fair, that the city might never be broken; and there, Phoebus, didst herd the sleek kine of shambling gait amid the spurs of Ida, the many ridged.

XXI, 442

To think of Poseidon and Apollo as two personages who acquired a divine status at some time between Laomedon's reign and the Trojan War doesn't ring true. And to suggest that Poseidon and Apollo represent a coral-like stone unique to the Dalmatian coast (quarried on the island of Brač), which is soft when cut into blocks and hardens when left to dry in the sun, doesn't ring true either, as the wall has no such stone in it. The answer must then be that Poseidon and Apollo represent the alluvial silt of the plain (used to fill and level off the area enclosed by the walls) as when:

> . . . of all these [tributaries of the Scamander] did Phoebus Apollo turn the mouths together . . . And the Shaker of Earth . . . was himself the leader and made all smooth along the Hellespont, and again covered the great beach with sand . . .
> Thus were Apollo and Poseidon to do in the aftertime . . .

XII, 24

For the most part, the walls appear to be intact with the exception of the southwestern face, which betrays a restoration and the addition of a round tower in much later times.

10. SANIDE GATE

The northwestern face of the walls overlooks the Scaian Gates and is broken at the middle, directly opposite the Central Avenue, by an entrance to the enclosure within. One might suspect this entrance to be the one mentioned when Hecabe exits from the Thalamos Treasure Chamber, laden with her best offerings for Athene:

*Now when they were come to the enclosure of Athene on the city
height, the doors [thýras] were opened for them by fair-cheeked
Theano . . . for her had the Trojans made priestess of Athene
. . . Then with sacred cries they all lifted up their hands to
Athene; and fair-cheeked Theano took the robe and laid it upon
the knees of fair-haired Athene . . .*

VI, 297

But these doors must be some other ones entrusted to Theano, for
Hecabe was *already*:

. . . come to the enclosure of Athene on the city height . . .

ibid.

and therefore, a description of this gate must be the one given by
Polydamas:

*". . . the city shall be guarded by the walls and the high gates
[hypselaí te pýlai] and the plank-doors [sanídes] fastened
together [epí tes araryíai], large, well-smoothed, fixed-fast,
bolted shut."*

XVIII, 274

as one with planks glued, or nailed, but 'fastened together' and 'fixed
fast' into the masonry, and far too heavy for Theano to move.

11. PLACE OF WATCH

One enters the enclosure within the walls through the Sanide Gate and
comes onto a court. Thence, turning to the right, one passes a winged
Lion of St. Mark.

At the western corner of the walls, overlooking the Scaian Gates, is a
vantage point which offers an almost unrestricted view of the Troic
and Ileian Plains. Roman (or Byzantine?) remains of a structure suggest the tactical value of this place, for it was here, that:

*. . . they that were about Priam . . . sat as elders of the people
over the Scaian Gates . . . like unto cicalas that in a forest sit
upon a tree and pour forth their lily-like voices, even in such
wise sat the leaders of the Trojans upon the wall.*

III, 149

This belvedere was the place to which Helen was called, and asked to:

"*. . . sit before me* [Priam], *that thou mayest see thy former lord and thy kinsfolk and thy people . . .*"

III, 162

who were assembling on the nether side of the Troic Plain.

12. TEMPLE OF ATHENE

Towards the southern corner of the walls is a cluster of ivy-covered ruins of fortress-like proportions evoking a Roman character. One can notice the buildings were once a part of the round tower incorporated into the walls. After passing through a maze of rooms, one comes unto a garden-like grassy avenue, flanked on the left by the ruins and on the right by a lush growth of trees, and thence onto a reticular set of plots running parallel with the northeastern face of the walls before coming back to a care-taker's house and the court in front of the Sanide Gate.

Somewhere within the mass of these ruins was the Temple of Athene, and only an educated guess can make a plausible conjecture of what it was, until archaeological information can be retrieved.

The temple was a *naós*:

> *Now when they were come to the enclosure* [neòn] *of Athene in the city height, the doors* [thýras] *were opened for them by fair-cheeked Theano . . .*

VI, 297

The sense is that of a *nave*, or a dwelling place of a deity, hence a 'temple,' but not necessarily denoting a covered place, so the idea of an *enclosure* as an area restricted within the walls 'in the city height' is sufficiently accurate. And given the generally watery associations of Athene with places such as springs, wells, sources of rivers, marshes, and the like, and the phallic homology of her enclosure on Callicolone, one might easily suspect her temple may have been a sacred well, or reservoir of some sort; or, on a cue with Hecabe's propitiatory offering of her finest robes, perhaps even a tannery?

13. THEANO'S GATE

The idea of a watery precinct for Athene's temple is strengthened even further by the existence of a cloacal drain, once servicing the heart of the fortress-like ruins where the temple should be found, which exits at the southeastern face of the walls. This drain will have necessarily been fitted with a sluice gate of some sort (if the idea of Athene's temple is on the order of a tank or reservoir), and would account for:

> . . . *the doors* [thýras] . . . *opened for them by fair-cheeked Theano* . . .

loc. cit.

which, in turn, suggests that when:

> . . . *fair-cheeked Theano took the robe and laid it upon the knees of fair-haired Athene* . . .

VI, 297

the image of Athene—whatever it was—was to be found in muck and slime at the bottom.

What seems remarkable—and more than merely a remarkable coincidence—is that when Gabela went under the name of Drijeva, it was the centre of a salt market . . . a tradition perpetuated by its own inhabitants?

APPROACH TO ROOMS OF ALEXANDER FROM THE PROTHYRON.

VIEW OF [SCAIA] FROM THE SANIDE GATE.

PLACE OF WATCH WHERE ELDERS SAT OVER SCAIAN GATES.

SOUTHEASTERN CORNER OF WALLS ON CALLICOLONE.

PART IV

CHAPTER 7

THE NON-MYCENAEAN HERITAGE OF HELLAS

Parting from the premise the *Iliad's* geographical information is sound enough to establish a positive identification of Ilios with the town of Gabela, what sort of an historical background can be inferred from the rest of the *Iliad's* geonyms?

The inherent difficulties in a thesis of a Dalmatian Troy are tantamount to a phenomenal confusion of seemingly contradictory historical facts. And perhaps—in the name of truth, and for its sake—things had better stand as they have. But then, as the validity of the Homeric Position is indestructible, there is no alternative but to examine the problem with diligence and offer a cogent structure for a fluent and cohesive chronology.[1]

A simplistic picture for the cultural origins of Hellas—the mainstream of its language, myth, religion, technology, customs, and so on—makes a Greek national character emerge with the inherited remains of a former Mycenaean civilization. It is within this framework that the great conundrum of the Homeric Question is set concerning the origins of the *Iliad* and the *Odyssey* and their questionable sense of historical validity. But this picture of Hellas' proto-history is factually distorted and historically anachronic. One might say that, by extension, the current sense of reality in Hellas' obscure proto-history

---

1. Still another, more serious, difficulty is the implication that the great luminaries of the entire corpus of classical literature—those who were, ostensibly, well informed—were utterly ignorant of the Homeric Tradition and its historical significance. Yet, one wonders whether this implication is not illusory and, whether or not, one has simply failed to read between the lines of a text with sufficient caution, and missed its intended meaning or misjudged its historicity.

A COMPARATIVE CHRONOLOGY

B.C.	ILLYRIA	HELLAS	ASIA MINOR
?	NEOLITHIC PERIOD Aboriginal communities occupy isolated parts of mainland and islands.		
1400	PROTO-TROJAN PERIOD Neolithic peoples begin to crystalize as Trojans. Cadmos Dardanos Tros Ilos	MYCENAEAN CULTURE (Heroic Age)	
1300	Trojan Period Laomedon		Hittite Letters
1200	Orpheus Trojan War	SUBMYCENAEAN PERIOD	
1100		Dorian Invasions PROTOGEOMETRIC PERIOD Ionian Migrations	TROY VIIb2
1000	Compositions of *Iliad* and *Odyssey*, and other works no longer extant.	**DARK AGE**	
900	EARLY ILLYRIAN PERIOD	GEOMETRIC PERIOD	
800		Lycurgus	
776	MIDDLE ILLYRIAN PERIOD Illyrian incursions abroad.	First Olympic Games	
750		EXPANSIONISM Homeridae tour Hellas. Transference of Homeric nomenclature to Hellas.	
700			Foundation TROY VIII
650		**ARCHAIC PERIOD** Peisistratean recension of *Iliad*	

is just as vague as a reader's studious efforts of linking a mental to-pography of Troy with the reality of the existing terrain of Asia Minor.

Whereas some Mycenaean influence, welded with traits of the Dorian Invasions from the north, cannot be precluded from the forma-tion of a general character of Hellas, the historical elements of Greek myth (the period known as the Heroic Age) from which a picture of Mycenaean times is erroneously adduced, had its roots and scenarios in Italy which, for some reason or other (tentatively explained in the following chapter), became Grecized at a later date.

The word 'myth' was first coined by Homer. Its sense is that of an *order* of things, of an *orderly story*. A myth is not just a story taken from the folksy imagination, or a story which survived because it was a good one to remember, but rather, a story which was developed along certain lines and constrained by certain parameters; it is, if you wish, a tightly controlled 'parable.' A myth might be likened to a postage stamp: it has a value and an age, and the story in its picture may be pristine or faded. And the current state of Greek myths—for the pur-pose of glimpsing into the life and times of ancient societies—is like a young boy's cigar-box full of unsorted stamps which require the careful process of classification by country, age, value, and so on. Some myths are good, that is, they are basically sound, because some historical sense can be discerned when they make a point of contact with geo-graphical reality. Other myths are bad, that is, they are intrinsically useless, and may be thought of as historical aberrations.

A fact that I suspect about the general body of Greek myth is that, rather than being a random collection of independent stories about local incidents which developed into a sophisticated language of myth (that is, became formal myth), all Greek myth, to a greater or lesser extent, impinges exclusively on the proto-history of Troy. Somehow and somewhere in Troy, it filtered into an existence as a full-fledged, formal genre of literature. And because the language of myth is a poetic language, its existence will have had an ulterior religious func-tion, not unlike the biblical stories in the Testaments of our Judeo-Christian tradition.

Of the earliest myths is the story of the Cretan prince Scamander who gave his name to the great river flowing through Troy, and his youthful traveling companion Teucros, the eponymous ancestor of the Cretans. There are several versions, now all garbled, but one espe-cially interesting note is to be found in Lycophron (4th c. B.C.), who says in his *Alexandra* 1303:

> . . . [the Cretans] sent with Teucer and his Draucian father
> Scamandrus a raping army to the dwelling place of the
> Bebryces to war with mice . . .

Draucian, meaning 'necklaced,' perhaps should invite an interpretation that Scamander and Teucer made their way into the Adriatic from
the east, via the Danube, and thence the Dravus, one of its upper tributaries. Perhaps they were known in Lycophron's circle as personages
indentified with a land-locked Central European people who expanded
their borders beyond the Dravus, and to be identified by modern
archaeology as an Iron Age people representative of the Hallstatt
culture. The Bebrycians, or 'Gnawers,' were a local Trojan tribe,
and have traditionally been regarded as a mouse-totem people. Strabo
(2nd c. B.C.), in his *Geography* XIII, i, 46, wrote about them:

> When the Teucrians arrived from Crete . . . they had an oracle
> which bade them to 'stay on the spot where the earth-born
> should attack them . . .' by night a great multitude of field-mice
> swarmed out of the ground and ate up all the leather in their
> arms and equipment; and the Teucrians remained there . . .

But Strabo, in his characteristic quest of meditated misinformation,
is referring to Chrysa on the island of Zacynthos which means 'very
dog-like,' so called because it was overrun by hordes of mongoose. But
the Bebryces were a mainland, not an island people, and that they
should have been an earth-born people and attacked their enemy by
night, points in the direction they were a mole-totem people, which has
a bearing on the identities of Scamander and Teucer.

Now, the Cretan prince Scamander, and Teucros the eponymous ancestor of the Cretans, did not come from Crete to Troy, but rather, went
from Troy to Crete. Also, they are likely one and the same personage,
the names of which are used solely to avoid confusion, and distinguish
the respective adventures or labors performed in Troy and Crete.

The name of Crete is consigned in the *Catalogue of Ships* with those
of seven other places, and is to be identified with the place that later
became known as Rome. Its Homeric epithet is *hecatómpolis*, 'a hundred cities,' which must be an early editorial correction from the otherwise better sense of *catacómpolis* or *catatómpolis*, 'city of catacombs' or
'catatombs.'

It seems then, that Scamander sought a place beside a river, van-
quished its mole-totem people, and named the river after himself. It
was later said the Scamander's waters could impregnate women who

bathed in them; but this is a ruse to account for the river's prolific number of conger eels, and at the same time, make Scamander the ancestor of the Trojans. Afterwards, under the name of Teucros, he sought another place beside a river, called it Crete, and its people Cretans after himself, and emulated the Bebryces with a vast network of labyrinthine tunnels.[2]

There is still an important element missing from the story of Scamander, alias Teucros: if Teucros began an important set of earthworks in Crete, what did Scamander do in Troy, other than vanquish a people and name a river? Since the name Crete is that of a site, and not like that of Troy, the name of a country, then conversely, Scamander's association should be with the site of Ilios. This invites speculation that he designed and built its oldest earth-works, the megalithic observatory on the western spur of Gabela which date from neolithic times. A little imagination easily pulls the name of Sisyphos as a viable candidate for setting up the stones of a megalithic observatory. Indeed, an icon shows him pushing the perfectly round disk of the eternally shifting sun into position atop a hill, and surrounded by little winged Keres meant to be read as malaria-bearing mosquitos.

It seems then, the story of Sisyphos and the Keres may have been a local Trojan story which evolved and became Scamander and Teucros. They may have been, rather than like father and son, identical twins, and the seed of the later stories of Romulus and Remus.

The name of Crete survived through subsequent centuries, until the beginnings of the Iron Age, circa 860 B.C., when it changed to that of Rome. The story of the foundation of Rome in the myth of Romulus and Remus evidently reflects a social change, or disturbance, and accounts for other, earlier dates than the traditional 753 B.C. for the foundation of Rome.[3]

Now, another myth independent of the story of Scamander and Teucros (taking place shortly afterwards), is that of a certain Cadmus who was sent by his father Agenor[4] in search of his sister Europe.

---

2. An educated guess for the foundation of Homeric Crete may be circa 1,600 B.C., signaling the opening of the Bronze Age. The story of Theseus and the Minotaur, just prior to the Trojan War, may reflect the recent Bronze Age, circa 1200 B.C.

3. That Virgil sentenced Aeneas to wander ever in quest of his ancestral land of the Teucrians suggests that Virgil and his contemporaries were well acquainted with another, older tradition regarding Rome's Trojan ancestry which differed considerably from the more popular views of the day that made Romans descended from Aeneas through his son, Ascanius.

4. Agenor the Elder, father of Cadmus, and founder of Patavium (now Padua) is grossly confused for Agenor the Younger, a Trojan prince, founder of Pardua (now Stonski).

She had been abducted by Zeus in the form of a bull and carried away—by sea—to Crete (that is, Rome), where she bore Minos and Rhadamanthys. Cadmus traveled to Boeotia, the country up-stream the Po, and thence, came to rocky Pytho of the Phocians, on the Tyrrhenian Sea (not Delphi, as the stories read, which in post-Homeric times was said to have carried the former name of Pytho).[5] There he came into some sort of confrontation with the Phocians, for he slew a dragon (perhaps a sacred seal, which had carried Europe on its shoulders to Crete, and not a bull, which will have had to use a land route). Cadmus gathered the dragon's (or seal's) teeth, returned to his native land, sewed them in the ground, and from these were sprung the Spartoi, ancestors of the Spartans.

These special, magical teeth from rocky Pytho, were some sort of stone—perhaps a mollusk to which the seal was partial? and from which Tyrrhenian (not Tyrian) purple was made? or stones employed by seals to break open a mollusk?[6] Whatever they were, they were taken back to Cadmus' country at the Adriatic's headwaters, and there became associated with the birth of the Spartoi.[7]

In the *Catalogue of Ships*, Sparta is a district-type name assigned to the country between Trieste and Venice. There, the outstanding topological feature striking one's eye is the drainage of the uplands through stony river-beds strewn with rounded boulders of all sizes, running parallel and close to each other, like the teeth of comb, into the Adriatic.

It becomes apparent that Leda's Spartan children, Castor and Pollux, were fathered by a large bird (and a swan is apt enough) to account for their autochthonous origins, like the Spartoi, in the country of egg-like boulders; and if Sappho's lines (J. M. Edmonds, 97):

---

5. Rocky Pytho (so called in the *Catalogue of Ships*) is to be identified with the corniche south of Genoa; a (pseudo-)Homeric Hymn associates the name with the death of a Dolphin (whence the erroneous association of Delphi with Pytho?) which changes from one set of beautiful colors to another, the instant it begins to '*putrify*.'

6. The idea of Tyrhian purple (though in this case, Tyrrhenian purple) involved in the killing of a Phocian dragon is not too far fetched, and begins to make some geographical sense as soon as one understands that Sidon, where Paris obtained the beautiful robes that Hecabe offered to Athena in an act of sympathetic magic, is located in Phoenicia, to the south, and to be identified with Telamonia, between Casos and Cos, the later Popelonia and Cosa; these place names have a distinct association with 'cloth.' A version of the Cadmus story makes Europe not his sister, but the daughter of his brother Phoenix; the name is thought to have an etymological kinship with 'red'.

7. Loose teeth dreams, as Freud discovered, are associated with castration anxieties; the association of teeth with seed, in the instance of Cadmus, seems to go back through Agenor to Near Eastern origins, where the jaw-bone of an ass (that is, teeth) is intrumental in the murder of Abel for the descent of man through the line of Cain.

> They say that once upon a time Leda found hidden an egg of
> hyacinthine hue . . .[8]

are poetically accurate, they were born from hollow geodes, whose
inner surfaces are lined with hyacinthine-hued crystals.

Cadmus left the Adriatic headwaters and went to Illyria, where the
memory of his exploits is cherished to this day. He came to the place
earlier settled by Teucros, evidently still in search of Europe, and mar-
ried Harmonia (to whom he gave a necklace), brought concord to the
warring tribes of Encheleians and Bebrycians, adapted an alphabet to
the language of the day, founded Thebes near Ilios, and upon his death,
became a mottled stone snake. Here already, in the story of a conflict
between Encheleian 'eels' and Bebrycian 'mice' (or moles) settled by
Cadmus, is the stuff in the children's allegory of *The Battle of the Frogs
and the Mice*, which ends when crabs arrive on the scene (the crab
being a well known symbol of rejuvenation and concord) to lop off the
offending mice's tails, and thus turning them into moles.

By and by, there came to this land a certain Dardanus, a Thracian
from Cortona in central Italy. Again, there are several accounts with
a great number of details, all at variance with each other. However,
the general outline of the story should read that Dardanus settled in
the land which took his name, and afterwards swam across, rather
than walked, from the Hellespont to Samos, where he instituted the
Samothracian Mysteries.

The mysteries (so called simply because they were held secret from
the doctrinally uninitiated?) embraced orgiastic cult-rites of the
Thracian Dionysus. But another, subtle, element laced throughout the
mysteries—and perhaps their medullar essence—was the knowledge
of writing that Cadmus had established. It would seem that a connection between Samos and Thrace, whence the name Samothracian, was
linked by virtue of Dardanus' origins; yet, what appears to have
cemented the bond was a knowledge of writing, current somewhere in
central Italy, perhaps possessed by Thracians, or by their neighboring
Mysoi who were subservient to the Muse. (Later, the literary concept of
an 'Odyssey,' written after Odysseus returned to his native Ithaca situated on the southern slopes of Samos, can be traced to these environs.)

The Dardanians—adepts of the Samothracian Mysteries, as dis-

---

8. The exquisiteness of Sappho's lines is in the Aeolian pronunciation of *hyakinthinon*
as *uakinthinon*, thus making 'hyacinthine' an onomatopoeic word suggested by the hollow sound made by a geode's two halves when fitted together, like the clapping of cupped
hands.

tinguished from other local tribes who were not—acquired an enormous advantage over other peoples, for simply, the boon of writing is knowledge, and knowledge is power. And because the Samothracian Mysteries prospered—and one should think of political and economic terms—the cult underwent many changes.

Dardanus had a son, Erichthonius:

> . . . who became richest of mortal men. Three thousand steeds had he that pastured in the marsh-land; mares were they, rejoicing in their tender foals . . .

XX, 215

Erichthonius built the temple of Athene on Callicolone and then emigrated to Apulia with his horses, where horse-lore became prevalent;[9] his name, which means 'wool of the ground,' is an allusion to the hairy tarantula native to Apulia. He founded Athens at the site of the salt-marshes later known as Tarentum, whence Athene's Homeric epithet is *tritogeneia*, that is, 'born from Triton (the sea),' or 'born from *three* (salt marshes of Tarentum).'

Now the stories of Theseus and the Minotaur begin to make some historical sense. It appears the Minotaur's demand for an Athenian tribute of youths is related with the bull's original rape of Europe. And the reference in the *Iliad* to Ariadne's dancing court (perhaps an interpolation , but nevertheless a valuable one), whose name means 'spider,' links these youths with an Athenian tarantella, induced by the tarantula's painful bite.[10]

Erichthonius had a son, Tros, whom a post-Homeric tradition made a native of Troezen near Athens (modern Tricase), hence the Athenian boast of early Trojan kingship.

And Tros had a son Ilus, after whom, it is said, Ilios was named. But on cue with *Genesis*, IV; 17:

> Now Cain had experience of his wife, who conceived and bore Enoch. He was the founder of a city, and he named the city after the name of his son Enoch.

Tros will have been the founder of a city and named it Ilios after the name of his son Ilus, who, in turn, will have named the country Troy, after the name of his father, Tros.

---

9. *A* (intensive inseparable prefix) + *polos* 'young horse.' Hence Apuleius, of Tarentine extraction and author of the *Golden Ass*, called himself an Athenian.

10. Is it possible the tarantula bite was inflicted as an act of sympathetic homeopathy to cure St. Vitus' dance?

Ilus had a son Laomedon, who built the walls around the perimeter of Callicolone. They were the last works to be done to the site of Ilios; and this act, which finally consecrated Ilios as a cult-shrine, might be thought of as closing the canon of Troy's early history and the opening of a new phase, by the full consolidation of the Samothracian Mysteries represented in the arrival of Orpheus at Troy (from whom, eventually, Homer would be descended).

An aspect of this new phase of Trojan history is that the Heroic Age came to an end with the Trojan War. Little, if anything, of myth survived and continued into post-Trojan times; to all intents and purposes, the quasi-historical information of myth stopped or, to put it another way, events were no longer recorded in the poetic language of myth. On the one hand, one might say there were no more heroes about whom stories could be recorded: that an established order of society had collapsed into a state of local petty tribal whims, and these offered no material for myth-making. But on the other, one might also say that, because myth stopped suddenly, this reflects its willful suppression —the end of a canon—and that because myth is a *kind* of a topic, a genre, it is now nothing more than the scattered remains of a no longer extant formal literary work.

Orpheus arrived with the expedition of the Argonauts and stayed on, while the rest continued northward hugging the coastline. It is said his demise was on account of orgiastic Maenad women who cut him to pieces, and that his head floated, singing, to Lesbos. But the story should read that he attempted swimming to Samos (not unlike Dardanus before, or Odysseus after him) from Lesbos, but instead met his death after foolishly seducing lesbian Lesbids with his songs.

No sooner had Podarces, son of Laomedon, assumed kingship under the name of Priam, than Ilios was destined to destruction. It enjoyed the benefits of prosperity only briefly, but since the site was a shrine rather than a city, it seems as though its fate now under the responsibility of Priam, was preconceived. And so Priam should be regarded as the first of many witnesses to systematically record the events of the Trojan War.

One cannot take the report of the Trojan War in the *Iliad* literally (and one doesn't, usually, what with the interference of divine beings in the affaires of mortals); and even the proposition of a conflict between Danaans and Trojans in the sense of a war must be viewed with caution, as both the account and the subject matter are mystical and smack of a sacred text and a cult-ritual. And then, there is the question of the *Iliad's* sense of 'historicity' (which tends to open a philosophical

discussion of what history is and is not), and just how much liberty has
been taken to accommodate 'the facts' as one would have them viewed:
for instance, that Homer makes a federation of Trojans out of a number
of Illyrian tribes, or that Homer assigns the Trojan seaboard such a
nomenclature as to unavoidably represent obvious phallic associations.
In this question of historicity, no one can really believe that Helen
alone was the cause of a war, for the two major thrusts against Troy
under the respective leaderships of Agamemnon and Menelaos were
forces conscripted from the southeastern and northeastern parts of
Italy. The boundaries of these territories, as represented in the *Catalogue of Ships*, conveniently form the shape of a three-legged, sun-
faced *trinacría*, and this shows that the political alliance between these
two widely separated (and even culturally different) territories was
strengthened by more than brotherhood, and that the Danaans' con-
certed effort in the destruction of Ilios was a ritual one.

The intellectual relevance of the various episodes of Danaans and
Trojans going to and fro over the Troic plain is that, given the particu-

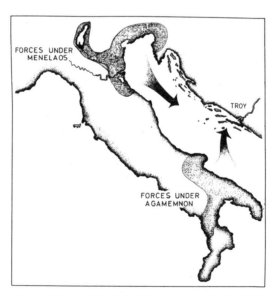

The *trinacría*-shaped boundaries of the countries held by Agamemnon
and Menelaos, leaders of the expedition against Troy, show that, according to the *Iliad*, there were ulterior motives of a religious nature for
the Trojan War other than the mere rescue of Helen and revenge for her
abduction.

larly marshy nature of the terrain, the rendering of the word *hárma*, an 'armature,' of 'that which is held together,' as 'chariot,' should be extended to understand that of a 'boat' weaving in-and-out amongst thickets and rushes, through a criss-crossing mesh of canals. Even today small, flat-bottomed boats are an integral part of life for those living along the marsh shores, and one might begin to think of spear-throwing from armature to armature as allegories of naval battles, laced throughout with some sort of literary secret. These battle maneuvers are far richer in the stuff of poetry than a mere 'dynamic narrative power of a superb story-teller . . .'

The *Odyssey* carries the name of Odysseus, simply because it is the narration of his adventures, and perhaps also because it was authored by Odysseus himself. Though the *Odyssey's* authorship has been strongly attached to the name of Homer—because it is in the same epic vein as the *Iliad*, and because certain internal points of contact with the *Iliad* point in this direction—it would seem that the real reason is because Odysseus was a Homer who wrote an account of his own adventures. And, since the personality of the *Iliad's* authorship, also ascribed to Homer, is different from that of the *Odyssey*, it is not unreasonable to suspect that the name of Homer is titular, as if, say, the name of 'rabbi' had, for some reason or other, been elevated to that of a person as the author of a number of writings, each betraying a personality, though ascribed to Rabbi.

The irony of the *Odyssey* is that Odysseus could have walked from Ilios to Ithaca in two days, or so. But because he betrayed Troy to Agamemnon by giving him a logistic *pied a terre* on the mainland (without which Agamemnon could not have launched the final naval assault recounted in the *Catalogue of Ships*), he was banished.

It was through Orpheus that a literary concept of an 'odyssey' was supplied to Odysseus. Some of his wanderings along the Dalmatian coast even trace part of the Argo's route.[11] But the idea itself of an Argonautic expedition was hatched in Iolcos, in the very heart of Thrace where Orpheus was from. Quite likely, it contained elements of another, slightly earlier, Odyssey-type story about the wanderings of one Tlepolemos, alias Ulysses, through Lindos and Ialysos and Cameiros (collectively known as Rhodes), which are to be identified with Sicily, Sardinia and Corsica, and who, it is said, went even as far

---

11. This discovery by Aristid Vučetić some three decades ago has recently been given extensive coverage in a lengthy series of articles published in the Yugoslavian newspaper *Politika*, as of July 24, 1983.

as the Ballearics, hence the mistaken identification of Odysseus with
Ulysses and the erroneous setting of the *Odyssey* in these waters.

The Trojans (as distinguished from other Illyrian tribes) were a fully
literate people. (Consequently, Homeric scholarship should have no
need of contriving the mechanism of an oral transmission to account
for the survival of the *Iliad* and the *Odyssey*.) And somewhere in Troy
was a repository of learning—a library, if you wish—but *where*? Several sites insinuate themselves with marked literary associations: for
instance, take Thebes, founded by Cadmus, or the Rooms of Alexander
where Helen wove the incidents of a war, like a Bayeaux Tapestry, that
was yet to be.

But perhaps, before asking a question of the following sort, one
must have a notion of an answer: the *Odyssey* speaks of rhapsodes
on Scheria, the tiny island of Scedro lying off the southern shores

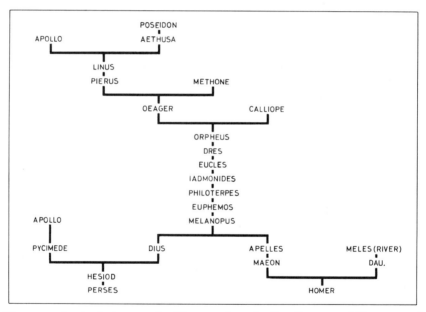

The genealogical stemma for Homer given in the *Contest of Homer and
Hesiod* connects him directly with Orpheus, and consequently with the
cult of the Samothracian Mysteries installed on the peninsula of the
Cephallenians. The stemma, rather than showing a blood-line, reflects a
chronological position for members of a college evidently associated
with the composition of the *Iliad*.

of Hvar, who may have been composing the initial draft of the *Iliad* while Odysseus was there; however, there is the question of whether Odysseus was not, in fact, drowning in the high sea and never on Scheria at all, but merely brought the idea of rhapsodes into his imagination from his recent exposure to them on the island of Ogygia; and the identity of Ogygia with Zacynthos, which became the classical Melita (now Mljet) neatly ties this island with an account of Homer's origins given in the *Contest of Homer and Hesiod*, making him descended on his father's side from Orpheus, and on his mother's, from the river Meles (that is, the many sweet water pools to be found on the island of Melita).

So it is (so briefly!), that neither the nomenclature in the *Catalogue of Ships* nor the myths of the Heroic Age can reflect, in the least, any status whatsoever of a Mycenaean civilization from which, as it is believed, Hellas was eventually descended.

CHAPTER 8

THE DORIAN INVASIONS
AND IONIAN MIGRATIONS

What little information we have about the no longer extant *Nostoi* invites speculation about the many difficulties encountered in the *returns* of the Trojan War heroes to their native lands in Italy. The general picture would be that of an altered state of domestic affairs, over which former lords no longer held power because of their lengthy absence from home, and of the reduction of order to the whims of tribal societies. 'While the cat's away, the mice do play . . .' so to speak.

In Hellas, the gradual collapse and disintegration of the Mycenaean culture (a period near Mycenaean IIIA1, *circa* 1,400 B.C., prior to the destruction of TROY VIIb2) was followed by the Dark Age period spanning from about 1,100 to 776 B.C., which is coetaneous with the stories about the Dorian Invasions that came from the general area of Illyria.

These illiterate Dorians, banded under the names of three tribes known as the Hylleis, Dymanes and Pamphylloi, ravaged what was left of the Mycenaean culture (represented by the Submycenaean Period in isolated parts of Hellas), and swept into the southern ends of Hellas, and thence across the Aegean, into the southern coasts of Asia Minor.

The stories about the Dorians seem contrived, especially their genealogical ties with the Heroic Age. It is easy to suspect they were a mixture of stranded Danaans and homeless Trojans, and their origins in Illyria are confirmed through the link of the Hylleis tribe with Hylos and Melite, after whom the Hylaikos (or Hylikos) harbor in Corcyra Melaina (Korčula) and the island of Melita (Mljet), were named.

According to the chronology of Eratosthenes, the Dorians came into Hellas about 1,100 B.C. Archaeological evidence credits them with the innovation of making iron implements, and one must posit they also brought a proto-Greek language which substituted the local Mycenaean as a *lingua franca*, together with their folk-lore, traditions, religious customs, and so on. Their knowledge of iron-smelting links them with Troy, attested by several Illyrian Iron Age settlements on the higher ground skirting the Neretva River valley-delta. Yet one searches in the pottery of the Protogeometric Period (which is a radical stylistic break from the earlier Mycenaean) for a hint of something Trojan, or some sort of echo from the Heroic Age, and there is nothing.

The stories of the *Return of the Heraclidae*, the children of Heracles, are identified with the Dorian Invasions. These stories are inconsistent with Heracles going to Illyria and his progeny returning to reconquer as the Dorian Invasions, and they have the phoney ring of an account made up to explain the Greek language brought from Illyria. Though a movement of a people moving into Illyria and returning later cannot be archaeologically substantiated, it would be proper to note that some exchange between a Mycenaean and an Illyrian people is evidenced by the discovery in Dalmatia of a gold funerary mask, similar to Schliemann's celebrated mask of Agamemnon.

B.C.	CHRONOLOGY ACCORDING TO ERATOSTHENES
1,313	Cadmos introduces alphabetical method of writing.
1,183	Palamedes adds letters to the alphabet. Fall of Troy.
1,103	Return of the Heraclidae (Dorian Invasions).
1,043	Ionian colonizations (Ionian Migrations).
884	Guardianship of Lycurgus.
776	First Olympic Games.

Then there happened an odd thing: in 1,043 B.C., the Athenians set forth as the Ionian Migrations to colonize the coasts of Asia Minor, north of the district already held by the Dorians. But the question is, *which* Athens was it that sponsored the Ionian Migrations? The Homeric Athens of Tarentum, mentioned in the *Catalogue of Ships*, or the yet non-existent Athens of Boeotia?

Archaeological investigation of the Boeotian Athens has shown the relatively peaceful evolution of a primitive community into a more sophisticated society that was spared the ravages of the Dorian Invasions which are evidenced in other sites throughout Hellas. At some time the site took the Homeric name of Athens, yet the archaeological search of remains that would attest to the reality in the stories of

Athens' watery origins at the bottom of nearby Lake Copais is, shall
one say, jejune?

Rather, the Homeric Athens of Tarentum, founded by Erichthonius,
was literally flooded with political events during the reign of Codrus,
when its land mass sank below the level of the Ionian Sea, which offered his son Medon the opportunity of instituting a system of arch-
onships on a new, 'more equal,' democratic basis of ruling at the site of
the Boeotian Athens. Thus, the migrating Athenians (indistinctly under Codrus or Medon) were received kindly at a site that would hence-
forward also be called Athens, perhaps because of an affinity with a
people of original Athenian stock who had been stranded at Troy, and
who had found their way to this place through the Pamphyllic branch
of the Dorian Invasions.

By 1,000 B.C. Hellas already possessed something that was not
originally her own: a Homeric place name, a cult of Athene, some

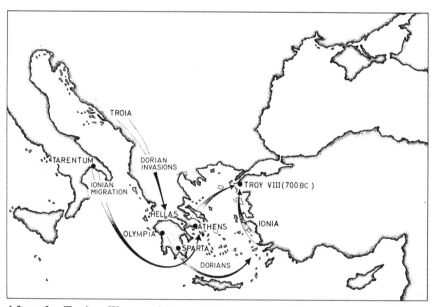

**After the Trojan War a mixture of Danaans and Trojans calling them-
selves Dorians penetrated Hellas from the general area of Illyria. They
were followed by Ionians who emmigrated from the Gulf of Tarentum
and settled in Athens. The western coasts of Asia Minor were later colonized by Hellasic peoples speaking Dorian and Ionian dialects. The
Aeolian dialect in the environs of Troy VIII was a late import of about
700 B.C.**

pretty important ancestries in the Heroic Age, and so on. Athens, to be sure, was the first to bring into Hellas a link with the past, for it could be reasoned that a certain Tros, son of a legendary king Erichthonius, had gone to a place which he named Troy, and later, Athenians had gone there to justly conquer it for themselves . . .

By 900 B.C. The Protogeometric Period of pottery had evolved into the Geometric Period (which again, can be regarded as a radical stylistic break), and one seeks something in this new period to elicit the memory of former times, and finds the following: the thesis whereby a correlation is sought between pottery of the Geometric Period and the *Iliad's* geometrical structure is set on the erroneous premise that its Greek authorship was coetaneous with this period. Instead, what would seem likelier, is that pottery of the Geometric Period may have had a source of inspiration from current labyrinth-lore surviving from the old Athens of Tarentum, and whence the concentric sense for the layout of the legendary Atlantis (and the fate of the trefoiled old Athens itself) may well have been suggested to Plato by some antique Geometric Period vessel.

By 884 B.C., Lycurgus founded the Spartan state as a political structure from the remnants of the broken-down Dorian community. That Sparta took a place name used in the *Catalogue of Ships* shows that already something of the history of former times was known locally. The name was evidently brought to Hellas by the Dorians, and so the question about the foundation of Sparta from a Pelopid line of descent must be ruled out as utterly anachronic, for the story is told that Lycurgus travelled to Troy, in search of advice regarding matters of legislation (where he evidently consulted those who had access to library information to set him straight) yet, what could he have found at the Asia Minor 'Troy,' where the site of Hissarlik lay abandoned from about 1,100 to 700 B.C.? An educated guess would make Lycurgus of Dorian extraction, and his line of descent (hence his right to figure prominently in the new Spartan state) from Theban ancestry, from the Thebes near Ilios, founded by Cadmus and the Spartoi.

The close of the Dark Age and the beginning of the Archaic Period, for which increasingly greater information becomes available, is reckoned with the establishment of the first Olympic Games in 776 B.C.

The mere existence of the games reveals several non-Hellasic ideas borrowed from Trojan sources. To begin with, there was nothing new about the Olympic Games, for they had been established before the Trojan War, and their only novelty was the name of Olympia in Hellas. It was borrowed from Olympos, not the mountain in northern Thessaly on the border with Macedonia, not yet so named, but from the Homeric

Olympos, which cannot be misconstrued in the literal sense of the text as a mountain. In Homer, Olympos is simply the dominion of gods and goddesses in the heavenly vault, and the intended sense underlying the name of Olympia was that of a place of similar god-like courses. Hence the *running* event was the central event in which humans evoked, or at least imitated, god-like qualities. The Olympian Zeus —that is, the Zeus whose temple at Olympia was intimately linked with the games—was simply an extension of the Zeus in the Homeric pantheon.

The institution of the Olympic Games continued successfully, indicating by all reasonable expectations, that Hellas was active in a world of travel and trade. It was now into the initial period of Expansionism and Colonization.

The chronology assembled for this period, from about 756 B.C. to the foundation of TROY VIII about 700 B.C., reveals by the use of some Homeric place names that some knowledge of the *Iliad* was already present. However, as the information for this period is collected from literary sources of many centuries later, it cannot be judiciously assumed that Hellas already possessed a full body of Homeric place names by that time.

CHRONOLOGY OF EARLIEST GREEK COLONIZATIONS

B.C.	HOMERIC	non-Homeric		HOMERIC	non-Homeric
756	**Miletos**		founded	**Cyzicus**	Trapezus
750		Greeks	colonized		Ischia
	Chalcis				Cumae
		Greeks	(factory)		Al Mina
734	**Chalcis**		founded		Naxos
733	**Corinth**		founded		Syracuse
730	**Eretria**		founded	**Methone**	Mende
729		Naxos	founded		Catana, Leontini
728		Megara	founded		Megara Hyb.
720	**Achaea**		founded		Sybaris
720	**Sparta**		conquered	**Messe(nia)**	
708	**Achaea**		founded		Croton
706	**Sparta**		founded		Taras
700		Sybaris	founded		Poseidonia (Paestum)
700		Aeolians?	founded	**TROY VIII**	

In the case of the Homeric Miletos, Achaea and Sparta, the name of Achaea may already have been part of Hellasic nomenclature by that time, as were Miletos in Asia Minor, and Sparta in Hellas. But the Homeric Chalcis, Corinth and Eretria read oddly—anachronously—and one must admit that what the original, non-Homeric names of these places were, are now lost to us. The use of the name Chalcis is especially queer: the sense in the chronology is obviously that Chalcidians from Euboea colonized Cumae and the island of Ischia sometime near 750 B.C., and this Chalcis is intended to be the Chalcis in Euboea listed in the *Catalogue of Ships*; however, another Chalcis is also consigned in the *Catalogue of Ships*, the one of the Aetolians, which is to be identified with the island of Capri (so called because of its shape like a foot-print, on a pun with the Latin *calx*, 'the heel' and 'lime, chalk'); it seems then, as though the author of our information on the colonization of Cumae, which is to be identified with the Homeric Olenos, is writing tongue-in-cheek and supplying us with *foul* information.

That this period of foundations and colonizations abroad by Hellasic towns may be archaeologically substantiated, is quite beside the point that the use of Homeric place names must be eyed cautiously, if only on the premise the Homeridae and the *Iliad* are likelier to have been a later, rather than an earlier, import into Hellas. In other words, it is difficult to pin-point an approximate date for the Homeridae's arrival in Hellas, and though an early date near the beginning of the Olympic Games cannot be ruled out, a later date sometime near the foundation of TROY VIII already begs for their presence.

So it is that Hellas gradually drew from former times for her own identity, and that a tradition of a former Heroic Age entered Hellas from abroad, and not as one would have it, handed down from within. Also, what could be construed as the remains of a former Mycenaean civilization yielding to Dorians and Ionians from abroad, should in fact be thought of as a bi-cultural heritage.

PART V

CHAPTER 9

THE ASIA MINOR 'TROY'

Some sort of explanation must be given to account for the Asia Minor 'Troy' and to understand what *motives* the Greeks had for identifying the site of Hissarlik with Ilios. At best, it rings with vested interests of a political ploy.

Somewhere in Hellas, or somewhere in Asia Minor, the Homeridae appeared on the scene with their rhapsodies. But where this occurred, is an idle question—perhaps at Olympia, to entertain a gathered crowd attending the games?—perhaps in some rich Ionian city where they could be afforded?

The delivery of the Homeridae's rhapsodies may have been something along the lines of the modern Yugoslavian *gušlar*, with an adaptation of the *Iliad* and *Odyssey's* hexameters to the demands of a *gušl*.[1]

What is certain is that a rote recitation of the *Iliad* and the *Odyssey*, in the form we possess them today, is not only highly improbable, it is impossible.[2] Here I must stress the importance of a perfect delivery, word for word, as opposed to a simply adequate delivery; the *Iliad* alone is such a delicate text, that the gist and punch-line—and the

---

1. The Yugoslavian *gušlar* recites from memory long epic accounts of ancient family feuds and the like, as he taps a foot in the metre of his recitation and strums the mono-toned lute-like, single-stringed (but sometimes two), *gušl*.

2. It should be clearly understood that a very special emphasis has been laid on the abilities of the Homeridae to deliver the Homeric Writings entirely from memory through the aid of multiple mnemonic devices of an oral tradition, simply because, hitherto, the hypothesis of an oral tradition is the *only* rational way of accounting for the *Iliad* and the *Odyssey* in the face of evidence that Hellas did not possess the knowledge of writing until after 750 B.C., or so.

beauty—of its lines, is dependent on the correct order of its wording.
But perhaps an audience might have forgiven a rhapsode a recrimina-
tion for delivering a line incorrectly, if and when the metre had been
spared. (The modern parallel is in that of a rabbi listening to a youth
misquote, and trip over the metre of *Genesis*; it may be close, but if it is
not word for word, it is not *Genesis*.) And, in addition to the enormous
difficulty of learning the entire *Iliad* and the *Odyssey* by memory, there
are the logistics of transmitting them in perfect order, from generation
to generation. An evaluation of such a proposition is easy: it cannot be
done! However, there is no reason for assuming the Homeridae may not
have delivered selected episodes, or specially condensed versions pre-
pared for an adequate delivery from memory (yet the proposition
smacks of a purist degeneration in the traditional relationship between the Homeric Writings and their absolute ownership by the
Homeridae).

The Homeridae's delivery of the *Iliad* and the *Odyssey* does not preclude written texts nor, it seems, of their reading parts directly from
them—in as many sessions as were necessary—for, owners as they were
of two sublime compositions,[3] there was no need for their wilful corrup-
tion through omission or condensation. A sort of theatrical production,
with characterization of parts and rhythmic accompaniment, seems
feasible and likelier to have occurred than to charge them with the
obligation of taking on an impossible task. But, for all an enraptured
audience knew, ignorant of the skill of reading, the Homeridae to
all intents and purposes delivered from what *seemed* to be the vast
resources of a prodigious memory—yet a keen observer could not have
failed to note a consistent relationship between a rhapsode's excellent
delivery and a text in his hands, and adduce that he was, in a certain odd manner, reading signs which aided him in drawing from his
memory.

The *Iliad's* impact on the Hellenes was of greater intellectual importance than that of first-rate entertainment. It may have been rowdy in
parts, and the *Odyssey* was even rowdier. But the *Iliad* was not for the
popular consumption of witless ears, for there was something intrinsic
that imbued it with a greatness far beyond its artistic value as a literary accomplishment: it was the priceless value attached to it by

---

3. The question of how many works the Homeridae owned, if other (no longer extant)
works attributed to Homer also belonged to them, would seem to imply the Homeridae,
more than just a travelling guild of rhapsodes, were a Trojan priesthood with exclusive
access not only to the Homeric Writings, but several other independent literary works
as well.

its audience—as men are wont to do—for its wealth of historical information.

No doubt, the *Odyssey* was also immensely appreciated. But by comparison, the *Iliad* was *bona fide*, all the way, and yielded more and sounder historical information. Through it—for those who felt the need of it—the present became tied with the utter ignorance of the past. One may even suspect the Homeridae wielded a measure of political influence, for the *Iliad* was accurate, and it was worthy of serious study, as it answered reliably all who asked interesting questions.

But soon, the no-longer guarded secret of reading and writing in the Cadmean method helped set the records straight on the excellence of the *Iliad's* authority, and settle claims, or legitimize remote ancestries, when and where so needed. Historical information about the antiquities of Hellas—genealogies, deeds, myths, and so on—spread in a flurry to the four winds.

Then! some scoundrel or other hit on a genial plan (truly a masterstroke in political chicanery): a Delphian's move to check the overbearing influence of Delos? or a righteous Athenian exulting in his city's pride of bearing in all Hellas the only name of a goddess? Whoever it was, and for whatever the reason, is no longer important. What happened is that the *Catalogue of Ships* was neatly lifted from its correct geographical context, and towns, ships, and captains—and with these all of the concomitant historical associations—were transferred to Hellas. The *Catalogue of Ships* became *the sole instrument that unequivocally vouched for the muddled memory of the past* as the supreme and incontrovertible authority on matters pertaining to the histories and ancestries of Hellas and its people in the Heroic Age.

For this purpose, all Hellas was formally renamed in an orderly, circuitous manner. The fraud, the malice of forethought, is self-evident in the comparison of a document which, on the one hand, represents a schematic distribution of peoples and places in Italy, and on the other, gives a sequential listing of peoples and places in Hellas in an orderly, circuitous fashion. Something reads oddly, for the implications are that the entire nomenclature of peoples and places in Hellas was lifted and arranged in such a manner as to give a neat schematic distribution of them up and down the length of the Italian peninsula, which is so preposterous as to leave one aghast! or that the other way around, someone had the preposterous audacity of using the *Catalogue of Ships* as a model for renaming *all* Hellas with Homeric place names!

Thus, as the explanatory footnote in the Loeb Classical Library edition of the *Iliad* notes:

The catalogue that follows enumerates the various contingents
which made up the Greek forces at Troy in the following geographical order: (1) those from the mainland of Greece south of
Thermopylae and from the adjacent islands; (2) those from the
islands of the Southern Aegean from Crete to Cos and the
Calydnae; and (3) those from Northern Greece, i.e. from the
region extending from Thermopylae to Mt. Olympos.

   The pilfering of the *Catalogue of Ships* and the eventual take-over of
the *Iliad* and the *Odyssey* from their legitimate owners was evidently
viable. This implies not only a strong political motivation, but also an
ulterior political gain. The history of Hellas had gone unwritten, and
rather than produce and export her own cultural traits, she borrowed
them from elsewhere and called them her own. But so much had been
borrowed that it became plausible—if not imperative—to revamp

**By 700 B.C. Hellas had borrowed so many of its cultural traits from
Danaan and Trojan sources that it became (politically) imperative and
(historically) plausible to revamp its nomenclature in an orderly, circuitous manner according to the sequential listing in the *Catalogue of
Ships*. This document became the ultimate authority to vouch for the
would-be authenticity of Hellas' origins in the Heroic Age.**

whatever was known of a haphazard history, and consolidate it in the form of the *Iliad* as a general Hellasic account of prior times. Within the next generation, the former names of places—whatever they may have been, and which are lost to us—now bore Homeric nomenclature, and with the nomenclature, the concomitant historical associations.

And so Hellas could now boast a history strung throughout with a common sense of cohesion.

And why not? The trumped-up stories about the *Return of the Heraclidae* confirmed that, upon a time, the proto-Greek language had gone from its native land, even as far beyond as Illyria, where the *Iliad* was composed in Greek. This was justification enough for claiming it, and the *Odyssey*, as patently Greek accomplishments, for only a tenuous, even an academic, difference could separate truth from falsehood.

However, the take-over of the *Catalogue of Ships* from the Homeridae, and its use as a model for the new nomenclature of Greece with all the derived benefits that went along, was inconsistent with a knowledge of an Illyrian Ilios. If anything, internal evidence in the *Iliad* made the take-over either an outright plagiarism and fall of its own weight, or the site of Ilios a geographically untenable and historically un-wholesome claim. Simply enough, there was no expedient way of reversing a memory of the earlier Dorian Invasions by northern peoples moving southward into Hellas, though perhaps the stories of the *Return of the Heraclidae* could be willfully misinterpreted to read a still earlier movement of Hellenes against Troy under the auspices of Heracles.

But a good solution to the problem would be the creation of a bogus Troy and a falsified location for the site of Ilios. A transference of an Italy-Dalmatia parallel could lend itself with credibility to a Greece-Asia Minor parallel. With some editorial doctoring of the *Iliad's* text here and there, and some minor details overlooked, it would seem that the *Catalogue of Ships* might stand up to scrutiny, after all.

The most plausible site for Ilios was in the northwest corner of Asia Minor, precisely at Hissarlik, where building materials were readily available from previous habitations. Here, enthusiastic colonists could revive the glory and splendour of former times. This became the archaeological stratum of TROY VIII.

By and by, an official text of the *Iliad* (and no doubt, one of the *Odyssey* too) became available for copying and, in passing, touched up here and there with an editor's zealous interpolation whenever needed:

And as the many tribes of winged fowl, wild geese or cranes or long-necked swans on the Asian mead by the streams of Caystrios, fly this way and that . . .

II, 461

So began a comedy of errors, and the further from the truth, the deeper the mystery, the greater the awe . . .

Now, as sublime as the Homeric Writings were, they were not necessarily the only truth. Nor were they, to some of those who understood them, so preponderant as to necessarily exclude conventional thinking. And woe betide us when the parameters of truth are put upon us for, as much as Homer was the ultimate source of historical truths, there was one—a certain Hesiod—who dared to think differently.

Hesiod was 'non-Homeric,' by definition, and perhaps even 'anti-Homeric.' One should see him as the product of prosperous times, representative of Greek colonialism and trade expansionism which allowed, among many good things, an 'avant garde' experimentation with literary unorthodoxy. That Hesiod was, by contrast with Homer, 'Hesiodic,' or 'anti-Homeric,' does not imply he lacked proper understanding of the Homeric Writings. Rather, he preferred stating a different poetic view of the world order. There is a (biased?) hint to this effect in the *Contest of Homer and Hesiod* (which Hesiod won) when Homer himself concedes that the mark of wisdom among men is (171):

To read aright the present, and to march with the occasion.

But Hesiod was historically voided—like a mule, with no pride of ancestry—for there was nothing in his legacy to fall back upon as a poetic source of information. There was not in Hesiod, as there was in Homer, the repository of *all* history. And as excellent as Hesiod's poetry was, he was still superseded by Homer, in that he borrowed literary techniques—writing in the Cadmean method, the use of the hexameter, and so on—from Homeric sources. Hesiod was a person, but Homer was an institution.

Hesiod's only redeeming virtue was the audacity of having stated that other poetic ideas were available. Yet the value of Hesiodic thinking, and the question of his sources of information that put the very Homer to test, were of such academic importance as to require splitting hairs and make him, centuries later, not only the winner of a contest but also associated with Homer through kinship.

This philosophical difference of poetic principles was to become transcendental in the Greek sense of historical thinking. It became a full-fledged schism represented by two schools of thought: on the one hand, the Homeric Tradition whose historical truths were the succinct testimonies of the *Iliad* and the *Odyssey*; and on the other, a pragmatic, expedient, Grecizing of Homer with the necessary invention of a bogus Troy in Asia Minor.

And this is as reasonable an explanation for the Asia Minor 'Troy' as I am able to give.

CHAPTER 10

A POST SCRIPT

There is no evidence that Homer was really blind. A Delian hymn of the Ionian school (in a literary form somewhat along the lines of the Homeric Tradition) mentions its author as a blind man from Chios, and the name of Homer itself is thought to be a pun on *ómma*, 'the eye.' But any explanation of Homer's blindness is as good as any other, and one that occurs to me, on the strength of an innuendo that he was an unkempt, filthy man, is that he may have become diseased with oncocercosis and eventually went blind.

By the time the *Iliad* was incorporated by Peisistratos as a regular event in the Pan Athenian Festivals, Homer's reputed blindness had already become symbolic of introspective poetic vision, not unlike that of Calchas, the Trojan Expedition seer, whose name is derived from *kalchaíno*, 'to make troublous and dark' or 'to ponder deeply.' However, the truth about Homer's blindness is that it was a case of reverse identity transference, cast on him by an enraptured audience which failed to see the *Iliad* in its correct geographical context, and utterly misunderstood it, though willy-nilly became irremediably *pledged* (cf. *omertá* of the Sicilian mafiosi) to its sublime excellence; and by so doing, gave a name to the otherwise unknown persons of its authorship.

The two main arguments of this book are the distilled efforts of two decades. On the one hand, it is simply the task of extracting the corpus of the *Iliad's* geographical information from the text, and finding a compatible geographical setting for it. And on the other, the task of working out a plausible historical frame for the concomitant implications and associations.

In retrospect, it looks easy. But let me assure the reader that it was not. Learning to think Homericly—in geographical and historical terms—was extremely difficult since, what so often seemed plausible (and in so many instances obvious) contradicted the weight of a classical tradition which, to boot, was so heavily endorsed by academia.

The question of archaeological 'hard proof' to substantiate the claim that Gabela is to be identified with the Homeric Ilios has come up, as if the results of trenching and stratigraphy could possibly settle the matter one way or the other. At worst, a thorough archaeological investigation of Gabela could only yield evidence for the same conclusion as is drawn from the evidence turned up at Hissarlik: this is not the site. And at best, archaeological investigation, desirable as it is, can only corroborate and enhance what was already known. Rather, the validity of what must be called the Homeric Position (the axiomatic identification of Gabela with the site of Ilios) rests with two rational arguments which, like the two sides of a coin, are the geographical setting for the *Iliad* in Dalmatia, and an historical frame for the concomitant implications and associations.

But, in my opinion, the embarrassing indictment is that if the *Iliad* is correctly understood in the context of its Dalmatian geography, and if a more-or-less satisfactory historical background can be worked out for the concomitant implications and associations, then one is left with the humiliating proposition there is a vast corpus of classical literature—a literary tradition of works directly and indirectly relevant to the Homeric Writings—that must be re-read for newer and better interpretations.

It is easily assumed that references to classical antiquities in classical authors, even when variant versions of this or that account are given, are to be understood within the general consistency of a homogenous historical tradition which, explicitly or implicitly, includes the premise of an Asia Minor 'Troy.' But this is short-sighted thinking, and nothing could be further from the truth. It simply cannot be said that all classical authors were commonly agreed that Homeric Ilios was in Asia Minor, regardless of the popularity of a tradition in its favor. Indeed, it is a grave mistake to think of classical literature as a cohesive body unanimously representing (or endorsing) the evolution of an historical tradition.

One must distinguish between those classical authors who were sufficiently well informed on their Homeric subjects, and those who bungled terribly. Strangely, on the face of it, no classical author really broaches the Homeric Question in depth, nor grapples with the problem in a direct way. The problem seems cautiously circumvented, and there even smacks the avoidance of an enquiry, as if the truth were a hushed matter.

But it is *precisely* that the truth was such a hushed matter which must be read into the works of the great luminaries of classical literature. On a pragmatic view of the matter, it is obvious that one of the problems a classical author faced when dealing with a topic associated with, or having a bearing on, the Homeric Writings was that the intellectual problem at hand was the setting forth of a statement, rather than entering into an indictment of the historical antecedents so that, whatever had to be stated, be correctly understood. That Homer had been Grecized was one problem, what had to be said, was another. It was understood the reader was expected to be at least moderately informed, and able to see through a particular author's lines and understand things which, certainly, have not been understood today.

The reader would be correct in assuming I suggest that modern classicism has reached an impass. It has become sterile and, like laboratory fruit-flies, so highly hybridized as to yield nothing of consequence in the future. But a *just* view of the matter is that modern classicism —its methodologies and techniques—is relatively new, and an ever-increasing number of scholars are participating in the fray of classical studies under the protective auspices of an ever-increasing number of institutions, unlike ever before. But modern classicism is not, unlike Church Dogma, without its blunders. Whatever mistakes have been made are logistically bound to be corrected sooner or later by newer findings. Academic blunders were necessary—they *are* part of a learning process—and this book could not have been written without them.

So, I shall now go and re-read all my *Loebses* . . .

A SELECT BIBLIOGRAPHY

A list of all the books which guided me, as points on a compass might guide a sailor, is tantamount to a pompous index of my entire library. And since this book was not designed to give the reader an account of a stream of consciousness, the bibliography given below merely represents a fair cross-section of those works which, like *prima facie* evidence submitted in a court, corroborate the axiomatic premise of the Homeric Position.

THE HOMERIC WRITINGS

Opera Homeri, 5 vols. Ed. David B. Monro and Thomas W. Allen. Oxford: Clarendon Press, 1963.

The Iliad, 2 vols. Tr. by A. T. Murray. The Loeb Classical Library. London: William Heinemann Ltd., 1965.

The Odyssey, 2 vols. Tr. by A. T. Murray. The Loeb Classical Library. London: William Heinemann Ltd., 1956.

HOMERIC SCHOLARSHIP

Bolling, George Melville. *The External Evidence for Interpolation in Homer*. Oxford: Clarendon Press, 1968.

Gordon, Cyrus R. *Homer and Bible*. Ventnor, N.J.: Ventnor Publishers, 1967.

Kirk, G. S. *The Songs of Homer*. Cambridge: Cambridge University Press, 1962.

Lord, Albert B. *The Singer of Tales*. New York: Atheneum, 1965.

Luce, J. V. *Homer and the Heroic Age*. London: Thames and Hudson, 1975.

Myers, Sir John L. *Homer and His Critics*. Ed. by Dorothea Gray. London: Routledge and Kegan Paul, 1958.

Nilsson, Martin P. *The Mycenaean Origins of Greek Mythology*. Berkeley, California: University of California Press, 1932.

Page, Denys L. *History and the Homeric Iliad*. Berkeley and Los Angeles: University of California Press, 1959.

Page, Denys. *The Homeric Odyssey*. Oxford: Clarendon Press, 1966.

Pocock, L. G. *Odyssean Essays*. Oxford: Basil Blackwell, 1965.

Vellay, Charles. *Controverses autours de Troie*. Paris: Société D'Édition "Les Belles Lettres", 1936.

Webster, T. B. L. *From Mycenae To Homer*. New York: W. W. Norton & Company, Inc., 1964.

Whitman, Cedric H. *Homer and the Heroic Age*. Cambridge, Mass.: Harvard University Press, 1967.

THE ASIA MINOR TROY

Alkim, U. Bahadir. *Anatolia, I*. Tr. by James Hogarth. London: Barrie & Rockliff, 1965.

Blegen, Carl W. *Troy and the Trojans*. New York: Frederick A. Praeger, 1963.

Cook, J. M. *The Troad: An Archaeological and Topographical Study*. Oxford, 1973.

Leaf, Walter. *Troy, A Study in Homeric Geography*. London: Macmillan & Company, Ltd., 1912.

Metzger, Henri. *Anatolia, II*. Tr. by James Hogarth. London: Barrie & Jenkins, 1969.

CLASSICAL AUTHORS

Apollodorus. *The Library*, 2 vols. Tr. by Sir James George Frazer. The Loeb Classical Library. London: William Heinemann Ltd., 1961.

Apollonius Rhodius. *Argonautica*. Tr. by R. C. Seaton. The Loeb Classical Library. London: William Heinemann Ltd., 1967.

Diodorus of Sicily. *The Library of History*, 12 vols. Tr. B. C. H. Oldfather. The Loeb Classical Library. London: William Heinemann Ltd., 1960.

Hesiod, The Homeric Hymns and Homerica. Tr. by Hugh G. Evelyn-White. The Loeb Classical Library. London, William Heinemann Ltd., 1954.

Lycophron. *The Alexandra*. Tr. by A. W. Mair. The Loeb Classical Library. London: William Heinemann Ltd., 1960.

Sappho. *Lyra Graeca*, Vol. I. Tr. by J. M. Edmonds. The Loeb Classical Library. London: William Heinemann Ltd., 1963.

(Pseudo) Scylax. *Periplus*. Jacob Gronovius, Leiden, 1697.

Strabo. *The Geography*, 8 vols. Tr. by Horace Leonard Jones. The Loeb Classical Library. London: William Heinemann Ltd., 1960.

Virgil. *The Aeneid*, 2 vols. Tr. by H. Rushton Fairclough. The Loeb Classical Library. London: William Heinemann Ltd., 1967.

CLASSICAL LITERATURE

Flacelière, Robert. *A Literary History of Greece*. Tr. by Douglas Garman. London: Elleck Books, 1964.

Graves, Robert. *The Greek Myths*. New York: George Braziller, Inc., 1959.

Pfeiffer, Rudolf. *History of Classical Scholarship*. Oxford: Clarendon Press, 1968.

GREEK HISTORY

Coldstream, J. N. *Geometric Greece*. London: Methuen, 1979.

Gordon, Cyrus R. *The Common Background of Greek and Hebrew Civilizations*. New York: W. W. Norton & Company, Inc., 1965.

Jefferey, L. H. *Archaic Greece, The City-States c.700–500 B.C.* London: Methuen & Co., Ltd., 1978.

Prehistory and Proto-History Ed. by Philip Sherrard and George Phylactopoulos. London: Heinemann, London, 1974.

Schefold, Karl. *Myth and Legend in Early Greek Art.* London: Thames & Hudson, 1966.

Taylour, Lord William. *The Mycenaeans.* London: Thames & Hudson, 1964.

GREEK RELIGION

Brown, Robert. *Schelling's Treatise On "The Deities of Samothrace".* California: Scholars Press, 1977.

Guthrie, W. K. C. *Orpheus and Greek Religion.* W. W. Norton & Company, Inc., 1966.

Mylonas, George. *Eleusis and the Eleusinian Mysteries.* Princeton: Princeton University Press, 1961.

Vermaseren, Maarten J. *Cybele and Attis, The Myth and the Cult.* Tr. by A. M. H. Lemmers. London: Thames & Hudson, 1977.

YUGOSLAVIA

Fodor's Modern Guides YUGOSLAVIA 1964 New York: David McKay Co., Inc., 1964.

Srejovic, Dragoslav. *Lepenski Vir.* Tr. by Lovett F. Edwards. New York: Stein and Day, Publishers, 1972.

Stipčević, Aleksandar. *The Illyrians, History and Culture.* Tr. by Stojana Čulić Burton. New Jersey: Noyes Press, Park Ridge, 1977.

Wilkes, J. J. *Dalmatia.* Cambridge, Mass.: Harvard University Press, 1969.

THE YUGOSLAV COAST, Guide Book and Atlas. Yugoslav Lexicographical Institute. Zagreb, 1966.

GENERAL REFERENCE

Genesis. Tr. by A. E. Speiser. Garden City, New York: Doubleday & Company, Inc., 1964.

Oxford Classical Dictionary. Oxford: Clarendon Press, 1966.

Bickerman, E. J. *Chronology of the Ancient World.* London: Thames & Hudson, 1968.

Burnbury, E. H. *A History of Ancient Geography* 2 vols. New York: Dover Publications, Inc., 1959.

Dasxurançi, Movses. *History of the Caucasian Albanians.* Tr. by Ç. J. F. Dowsett. London: Oxford University Press, 1961.

Piggott, Stuart. *Ancient Europe.* Edinburgh: Edinburgh University Press, 1965.

Thomson, Oliver J. *Everyman's Classical Atlas.* London: J. M. Dent & Sons, Ltd., 1961.

GENERAL INDEX